o End

Adoption Beginning to End

A Guide for Christian Parents

Donald W. Felker
and
Evelyn H. Felker

BAKER BOOK HOUSE
Grand Rapids, Michigan 49516

Copyright 1987 by
Baker Book House Company

ISBN: 0-8010-3537-6

Printed in the United States of America

Unless otherwise identified, all Scripture quotations are from the King James
Version. Those marked RSV are from the Revised Standard Version, © 1972 by
Thomas Nelson, Inc. Those marked NIV are from the Holy Bible: New
International Version, © 1973, 1978 by the International Bible Society. Used by
permission of Zondervan Bible Publishers. Those marked Phillips are from The
New Testament in Modern English, © 1961 by The Macmillan Company.

To
Bertha Elaine Felker
with affection

Contents

Acknowledgments

We would like to thank Doris E. Wheeler, Director, Thomas Idichandy, Director of Professional Services, Eleanor Hill, Coordinator of Community Education Outreach, of the Evangelical Child and Family Agency of Wheaton, Illinois. Their help in obtaining information from adoptive families is greatly appreciated.

We also gratefully acknowledge the contributions of the families of the Evangelical Child and Family Agency and other individuals who shared their adoption experiences with us.

Ms. Janet Baccene at the University of South Carolina entered multiple drafts of the manuscript into the word processor. Her help was cheerfully given and deeply appreciated.

Thanks are also expressed to the editorial staff of Baker Book House for kind and professionally competent help.

Don and Evelyn Felker

Introduction

This book is written for Christians who are thinking about adopting or have already adopted a child. It is also meant for those who are helping people make that choice, for older adoptees, and for members of the Christian community who desire to understand the adopting families among them.

When we began to consider writing a book about adoption for Christians, we asked ourselves: "Is such a book really needed?" Since we knew that book shelves were loaded with material about adoption, we did not wish to duplicate work already done. But as we began to read the available publications, we found many that were seriously out of date and very few approaching the adoption process from a Christian viewpoint.

We are passing through a period of rapid change in the field of adoption. Our own experience reflects the change. We have five children. Two of them joined our family by adoption. Our older son was adopted in 1959 and first came to live with us when he was four. He later spent a year with relatives, then returned to us with the prospect of adoption when legal barriers were cleared. His adoption was not typical for the period. Our friends who were pursuing adoption at that time were visiting agencies or finding babies privately and bringing newborns home directly from the hospital. Our younger son was adopted in 1970. He, too, was an older child who was already living in our home. His was an agency arranged adoption, but our friends who longed for babies were now finding themselves on long waiting lists. Financial qualifications and other requirements were being stringently enforced and many would-be parents were turning in desperation to finding their own babies.

The situation has continued to change dramatically. In 1970, nine of ten babies born out of wedlock were placed for adoption. Ten years later, nine of ten unmarried mothers were keeping their newborns, and the downward trend for available babies continues. By the middle of the seventies, researchers spotted a trend indicating that some of these children were coming into placement after several months or years of inadequate care. The dramatic increase in the use of effective birth control and the abortion explosion following the Supreme Court decision of 1973 have substantially lessened the number of infants available for adoption.

The reasons that couples consider adding children by adoption have also changed. Twenty years ago adoption was most often considered because of inability to produce biological children or because couples wanted to find a place in their family for a particular child. While those motivations are still important, adoption is frequently chosen today for other complex and varied reasons, some of them quite new. Some parents choose adoption in response to worry about population growth, preferring not to give birth to children in a world they see as already overcrowded. Others perceive certain classes of children as unwanted and adopt to provide a home for one or more of them. Adoption is sometimes used as a means toward fulfilling the dream of an integrated society or as a way to expose an established family to another culture. One naive woman suggested to me that they would adopt so she would not have to take time off from work to have a baby—and she had decided to look for one who was already toilet trained! This book will attempt to help you look at a Christian's motivations for adoption.

Adoption agencies have also changed. At one time some adoption agencies existed primarily to find babies for white, middle-class parents who were infertile. Today adoption agencies have as their goal finding the best possible home for a limited number of white infants and for a much longer list of children for whom placement may be difficult. Some agencies are screening out excess numbers of prospective parents who want only perfect white infants, and constantly searching for families who can be helped to parent an older child, an emotionally troubled child, a child with medical problems, or a sibling group. They are trying new ways to find minority-race families to adopt children who need homes within their cultural setting, and developing subsidized adoption and other financial resources to make adoption available to poorer families with parenting abilities.

Adoption has taken on an international aspect, and agencies are responding to the needs of children in other countries. The first of these children came to the United States when people became aware of the dubious place in Asian society given to children fathered by American soldiers overseas. New agencies were formed to handle such adoptions, and older agencies sometimes were asked to assist in follow-up of privately arranged international adoptions. Some people are asking serious questions as to the wisdom of importing children into American families rather than assisting those children within their own country. But the practice is continuing and extends now to children from many countries of the world who are not biracial, fueled partly by humanitarian impulses and partly by the acute shortage of white infants available for adoption in the United States.

Agencies are now charged with finding homes for children who formerly would have grown up in institutions or in foster care. Widespread belief that the impersonal aspects of an institution and the impermanence of foster care were bad for children has led to a movement to legally free these children for adoption and find permanent family homes for them. Although agencies once discouraged adoption by foster parents, now the foster family may be the first choice for a child who already has a place in that home. Because many of these children are older and badly scarred emotionally, they may be difficult to place elsewhere successfully. Children once considered unadoptable because of severe physical or mental handicaps are candidates for adoption today. Agencies are channeling much energy and substantial resources to locating suitable families, helping them adopt, and providing follow-up services for these special cases. We will look at agencies today, so that you can know what to look for in an adoption agency and how to work with them in adoption procedures.

Society's view of adoption has also undergone striking changes. Issues that once were handled almost solely by the agency, the family, and a fairly routine court procedure are now widely debated and subject to legal and social pressures. The question of children's rights has impacted upon the mechanism of adoption and raised a complicated set of legal questions, which interact with ethical concerns about the rights of children, parents, and society. What are the responsibilities of people who must make choices on behalf of children legally under their care? For example, when the Supreme Court ruled in a case originating in Illinois that the father of an illegitimate child has a right to participate in the legal process by which the child is freed for adoption, little attention was paid to the far-reaching consequences to children awaiting adoption. But the effects have been dramatic. Almost immediately the time in temporary care before placement of infants in permanent homes increased substantially. Other related issues have been raised. Whereas it was once assumed that the mother had the right to make whatever choice she thought was best for her child if she was not married to the father, now the father has been given an unclear legal role to play. These legal questions are part of what you need to know as you consider adoption.

Another set of new questions deals primarily with what is often called the Search (see chapter 9). These questions ask about the right of individuals to know their individual histories. For many years society regarded adoption as a final step that legally blotted out the past. Records were sealed. New birth certificates reflecting legal not biological facts were issued. Promises of confidentiality were given and kept. In some cases families chose to act as though the adoption had not happened—as though the child had in fact been born into the adopting family. In the seventies, spearheaded by articulate and forceful adult adoptees, a new movement developed. Its aim was to open adoption records and permit adult adoptees to know their biological heritage. Agencies, adopting families, birth families—and most of all adoptees themselves—are still struggling to find solutions to the Search that fulfill the needs and rights of all the participants. If you are considering adoption, it is an issue you must deal with, for some form of openness about adoption records seems certain to prevail legally and socially.

Prior generations frequently did not look at being parents as a matter of choice. If you chose sexual relations inside or outside marriage, bearing children was a natural consequence of that choice. Birth control by pill and other means has changed that. As more and more families see parenting as a choice, adoption becomes less unique, and every child becomes a "chosen child," to use the old way of describing adoption. Nor do couples need to find a way to adopt so as to appear "normal" in the eyes of society. We hope this book will help you decide if parenting adopted children is your choice—because you believe that it is *God's* choice for you.

In an attempt to meet the changing needs and unanswered questions of adoption, much new information has been made available. We have gathered statistical information on adoption outcomes. We know more about the kinds of problems parents are likely to meet and have an increasing body of knowledge from adopted persons as to how they felt about the process. Each of these sources of information is available to help you in your adoption choices.

The term *adoption* is used only four times in the Bible, but the adoption idea occupies a central place in the New Testament. Adoption is the method God has chosen to bring each of us into

the family of God. Because God has used this method for establishing his family, we have a viewpoint on adoption that is
uniquely viable for Christians. This book will look at adoption in
that light.

One of the biggest information gaps we found was lack of
materials that viewed adoption from a biblical standpoint. We will
explore information on adoption, changes that are facing prospective parents, issues that are being raised, and the mechanics
of investigating the adoption choice. We will try to bring all of
these into a biblical framework . An assumption of this book and
of our lives is that adoption is part of God's plan for nurturing
children in the Lord. Our aim is to help you think about, plan
for, and carry out adoption under the guidance and direction of
God's Word.

1

The Bible and Adoption

Understanding adoption from a biblical viewpoint is one of the central purposes of this book. The literature about adoption contains the expression "the adoption triangle," which usually refers to the baby, the birth parents, and the adopting family, or sometimes the agency, the baby, and the adults involved. Thinking about adoption biblically also involves an adoption triangle: God, parents, and children. We will look at Scripture to see aspects of God's nature that affect how we view adoption—to determine the nature of parenting presented in the Bible as God's standard or norm and to determine the scriptural view of children. As we see the biblical ideas about this adoption triangle, we will see how our own adoption into God's family through the Lord Jesus Christ models how children and parents become families through the adoption process today.

God in Adoption

The God of the Universe, who is infinite, eternal, and unchangeable in all his perfection, has chosen to reveal himself to human beings in the Scriptures of the Old and New Testaments. This revelation allows us to see him as he is and in a way that we can partially understand him. We know that he is the God and Father of our Lord and Savior Jesus Christ. This is one of the most dynamic ideas in the whole Bible! God wants us to know him and, in order that we may know him, he has identified himself as a Father! Many aspects of God we cannot fully fathom; others we barely begin to understand. But the fact that God is a Father strikes a note of harmony with our souls. Most of us have learned to love earthly fathers and mothers. Many of us have learned to be loving fathers and mothers and have enjoyed the dynamic relationship of love that develops between our children and ourselves. It encourages us to know that God pictures himself as having this kind of dynamically rich relationship with his people.

God Is a Parent

God invites us to pray to him as "our Father who art in heaven." There is a great deal of argument in our society about the sex of God. Is he a male ("Father") or is he without gender? Are we unjust to the daughters of God when we refer to God as a father? These arguments seem to miss the point of the scriptural image. God is referred to in the Bible both as a father and as a mother. The point at issue is not male or female gender but that he feels parental toward us and treats us with love and concern. These are emotions that good parents feel for the children given to them. "As a father pitieth his children, so the Lord pitieth them that fear him" is to teach us not that God is male, but that God regards us with pity and expects us to look with concern upon the needs of children and provide for those needs. In the scriptural picture, God's actions and emotions toward us are those of a parent who loves and nurtures. His actions set an example for our parenting.

God Is Merciful

Our wise and loving God-parent is also revealed as merciful. Children, widows, prisoners, sick, afflicted—all are the special recipients of God's concern. His mercy is shown by the fact that he commands special care for those who cannot care for themselves. Jesus began his public ministry by reading in the synagogue from Isaiah:

> The Spirit of the Lord is upon me because he hath anointed me to preach the gospel to the poor; he hath sent me to heal the brokenhearted, to preach deliverance to the captive, and recovering of sight to the blind, to set at liberty them that are bruised, to preach the acceptable year of the Lord (Luke 4:18–19; cf. Isa. 61:1–2).

Then he announced to the assembled congregation: "This day is this scripture fulfilled in your ears" (Luke 4:21).

Jesus tells us plainly that we will see in his ministry the merciful concern that God has for people who cannot care for themselves. In the broadest sense, this applies to all of us. We are the poor, blind captives who need to come to know the Lord Jesus Christ as our Savior and Redeemer. But it also has a further impact on how we view our responsibilities to minister in the name of Christ. Christian adoption must be shaped to be a ministry to those who need help.

God Is Sovereign

Another aspect of God seen in adoption is his sovereignty. As God determines what comes to pass and directs the course of human history, his mercy and love is worked out in the affairs of mankind. We sometimes speak of adopted children as "chosen," whereas we may use "planned" or "accidental" in referring to children who are born into the family. Scripture gives a different view. Where any child is born and where any child lives are God's choices. Whether conception is given or withheld, it is of the Lord. The Book of Hebrews tells us clearly that sometimes we face unhappy situations and that we should interpret even those in the context of God's mercy.

Birth is not an accident. The Scripture is full of examples wherein the birth of children is specifically shown to be the work of the Lord. Neither is adoption an accident. God uses the decisions, desires, and actions of men, but he is the one who is in control. One of the most comforting passages of the Gospels teaches us that principle: "Now if God so clothes the flowers of the field . . . is he not much more likely to clothe you?" (Matt. 6:30, *Phillips*). Jesus said that God has the very hairs of our head numbered, and a sparrow does not fall except by his decree (Matt. 10:29–30). Would something as important as the birth and life of children not be in his hand?

God pictures his loving sovereignty in these practical examples during the ministry of his Son Jesus. He also teaches us with sweeping declarations: "Yea, before the day was I am he: and there is none that can deliver out of my hand: I will work, and who shall let it?" (Isa. 43:13). As with our human limitations we painstakingly make our way through the choices and decisions of adoption, we can rely on the perfect and all-powerful love of God to accomplish his good will through us.

God Is Our Helper

One of the supreme blessings of life is that our Sovereign God offers himself to us as a source of help. When Peter was walking on the water, became scared, and began to sink, he cried, "Lord, save me" (Matt. 14:30). The parable of the woman who so persistently kept coming to the judge is given as a positive example to encourage us to persistently pour out our needs to God (Luke 18:1–8). These requests are brought to a God who promises to do exceedingly above all that we ask or think. Many difficulties must be overcome in the process of adoption. Many of you will confront other parents and children as they struggle to become a family and to mature together. In every circumstance our God is a God of help.

God Brings Good out of Evil

Our God is also merciful and strong in bringing good out of evil, and this aspect of his character is greatly significant in adoption. Many of the children available for adoption are born in painful, sorrowful circumstances. Some have birth defects, others have been permanently injured by wicked acts of abuse. The conception of a particular child may be the result of an unholy relationship. Adults in the situation may be either the victims or the doers of evil deeds that result in deeply sad situations. In all of these circumstances we can rely on God's ability to take that sinful, painful, or broken situation and bring into it his healing love so that good can come. Joseph said to his plotting, jealous brothers, "and God sent me before you to preserve you a posterity in the earth, and to save your lives by a great deliverance" (Gen. 45:7). Later he added, "But as for you, ye thought evil against me; but God meant it unto good . . ." (Gen. 50:20). The hatred of his brothers, the slavery, and imprisonment were not good; they were evil. But God brought good to Joseph and to many other people out of that miserable situation. Adoption often deals with people who are bruised and broken by sin, but God is merciful. Out of an unhappy, unwanted pregnancy can come a beautiful baby for a couple longing to be parents. Other examples abound, as we permit the healing, forgiving love of God to act in all the aspects of adoption.

Parents and Adoption

Just as God in his sovereign mercy has chosen to be a Father to us, so he has determined parenthood for us. Sexuality and sexual expression are a part of marriage, a beautiful gift from God. Conception is not an automatic outcome of sexual relations, but another gift from him.

Parenthood Is from God

The Bible is clear that conception is given or withheld by God's will. At the culmination of the love story between Boaz and Ruth we read: ". . . and when he [Boaz] went in unto her, the LORD gave her conception, and she bare a son" (Ruth 4:13). Notice that pregnancy did not just "happen." The Lord *gave* Ruth a baby. Isaiah 8:18 speaks of "I and the children whom the LORD hath given me," and the psalmist summarizes marriage, sexual union, and birth as "He maketh the barren woman to keep house, and to be a joyful mother of children . . ." (Ps. 113:9). Scripture does not speak of childbearing as "an accident."

Not only conception and birth, but adoption also is under the providence of God's will. Moses was spared and reared in the house of Pharaoh, and the Bible writers regard this as the hand of God moving in the drama of God's people. In the New Testament, the adoption process is used to picture our new relationship to God through Jesus Christ. The New Testament writers agree that this adoption process is under the direction and determination of God. He draws us, he makes provision for us to be his children, he sends his Son to redeem us, and he calls us sons and daughters in the family of God. All of this is summarized in Romans, Galatians, and Ephesians, where we find the only usage of the term *adoption* in the original language of Scripture. The word used is a dual word in the Greek that means "put as" and "sons." In the spiritual adoption process we are put into a new relationship. We are co-heirs with Christ and members of the family of God the Father. This is the model for Christian adoption. Like spiritual adoption, God puts us in this new relationship.

Parents Have Responsibilities

Along with the axiom that God gives parenthood is the corollary that parenthood carries with it responsibilities. Parents are to care for and rear the children they are given. If the circumstances do not permit them to fill this role (Moses again is a biblical example), they are responsible to assist in arranging for the necessary care. A biblical view of adoption must include both the parents, to whom God gave conception of the child, and grand-parents, who may still need to exercise some responsibilities toward a minor child who is a birth parent.

When the angel revealed their approaching parenthood to Samson's mother and father, they asked: "How shall we order the child, and how shall we do unto him?" (Judg. 13:12) These questions strike a familiar chord with first-time parents: "How are we going to raise this child? How are we going to know what to do?" Realizing that parents have a major responsibility for the children they are given makes parenthood a little frightening. Beyond basic physical needs, there is responsibility to "train up a child in the way he should go . . ." (Prov. 22:6). It is assumed throughout

Scripture that if a child is left to himself and is not given direction and guidance, the results will be poor and the child likely to go his own way into trouble. Proverbs tells us that a child left to himself brings his mother to shame (Prov. 29:15). A child without guidance is an indication of failure on the part of the parents to exercise care and correction and responsibility, which are all part of parenting. Timothy was blessed in that he had known the Scriptures from a child (2 Tim 3:15). The Greek word used here for "child" means "newborn" and gives the picture of a godly mother teaching her child the Word of God from the time he nursed until he was grown. A parent willing to accept this responsibility will find wisdom and help for the task freely given by God, who granted parenthood.

God places the responsibility of obedience to parents upon children, but as parents we must give close attention to the fact that we have the parallel responsibility to teach, to avoid provoking and discouraging, and to train them according to God's Word.

Patterning Our Parenting After God

The responsibilities we have as parents can be summarized as a commission to learn to parent our children as God is parenting us. In writing about specific topics, we will continually come back to this idea and explore its meaning. But let us begin to draw a picture of God's parenting as a model for ours. He does all things with perfection and we can only imitate him in an imperfect way, but copying God is a tremendous way to learn parenting.

God is an accepting and loving parent. The relationship that we have to God as his children is not based on our performance or on any quality within us that makes us attractive to him. The Bible is clear: God's love for us is conditioned only by the sacrifice of the Lord Jesus Christ and our being related to God through Christ. In Romans, Paul emphasizes strongly that it was "while we were yet sinners, Christ died for us" (Rom. 5:8). We frequently confuse our children by acting as though their relationship with us is based on whether they measure up to our standards. Behavior is important, but the standing of a son or daughter with his or her parents must be unconditional and based on God's acceptance and love for us.

The psalmist asked: "If thou, LORD, shouldest mark iniquities, O Lord, who shall stand?" (Ps. 130:3) Each of us could ask the same question about our relationship with our parents and with our children. If these relationships are based on "marking iniquities"—keeping track of performance and loving and accepting the person only if all is perfect—no parent or child would be able to stand the test. The psalmist says that the crux of the matter is God's forgiveness, in order that he may be reverenced. We want to pattern our parenting after God the Father and we must begin by accepting and loving our child in a relationship not bound up and conditional on the child's pleasing us or doing everything we want.

"Acceptance" is a broad term. What does it mean in action? Perhaps we can illustrate. Not long ago a happy mother of a sixteen-year-old adopted daughter told about the first few weeks of her child's life with them. Their daughter was ten months old when she was removed from foster care and placed with them. The child seemed to take an instant dislike to the mother. She cried whenever Mother entered the room, crawled into another room if possible, and refused to accept any mothering. She welcomed attention from her new father. Feeling rejected and dismayed, the parents called the agency to ask if they should return the baby. An experienced adoption worker responded immediately. She brought out the child's case record and went over it carefully with the parents. They realized together that the baby had been in three foster placements and that in each home the mother-figure was a long-haired blonde—as was her new mother. When she was able to accept the possible explanation that her appearance was somehow reminding the baby of her past experiences, the new mother realized that the baby's behavior was not a personal rejection of her. The mother wore a scarf for several weeks to hide her blonde hair and gradually the baby accepted her. She laughingly told me, "If she needed it, I'd have dyed my hair black to win her." Whether or not hair color was the key, the head scarf demonstrated acceptance of her baby as she was.

When a child is born into a family, the family has had nine months to begin to develop accepting love as the baby is carried and nurtured in the womb. That love cannot be based on performance by the baby! When a child comes into a family through adoption, unconditional acceptance and love must be consciously committed on the part of the new parents. If the child is beyond early infancy, there will probably be some characteristics and behaviors we would not choose our child to have. We have not seen the process in which those characteristics have developed out of interactions with the world. We have not had the experiences that show us that the child is "truly bone of my bone and flesh of my flesh" and is like us in failings, too. But we have experienced the free, unconditional love and acceptance God shows to us through Christ our Savior. His Spirit will help us commit ourselves to a free and unconditional love of our children, whether adopted or born into our families.

God is a parent who disciplines. Although God's love is not conditioned on our merit, he frequently acts toward us in ways that are based on our behavior. Keeping God's commands brings blessings, and failing to listen to the commands of God brings consequences that are unpleasant. It is one of the principles of the Bible that what a person sows he reaps. If we sow wild oats, we will harvest wild-oats consequences. But God takes no pleasure in the pain our sin brings to us. He uses the pain to help us. If we are suffering, the writer of Hebrews advises us to come to God and consider what he is doing in our lives. The discipline of God is designed to draw us to him. This painful experience is also designed to make us grow in Christ. Since God's discipline encourages closeness and growth, we need similar goals for disciplining our children. It should draw them to us rather than driving them away, and it should help them grow strong in the Lord.

When God disciplines us as children, two things stand out. First, his discipline involves both rewards and punishments. The Bible gives both promises and warnings. God's people are given encouragements to do good, along with warnings of the consequences of doing wrong. Our discipline of children needs a similar mix. Children need encouragement just as much as they need rebuke. They need rewards and blessings along with correction. We are counseled to bring our children up in the "nurture and

admonition of the Lord'' (Eph. 6:4). At times our own sinfulness
leads us to do one without the other. We either nurture and feed
and give good things and forget the admonitions or we go to the
opposite extreme. It is interesting that the nurturing or blessing of
God is usually placed first in his instruction. It should also be first
in what we do to and for our children.

The second outstanding characteristic of God's discipline of
his people is its individual fit. The psalmist said: ''Like as a father
pitieth his children, so the LORD pitieth them that fear him. For he
knoweth our frame; he remembereth that we are dust'' (Ps.
103:13–14). This statement appears at the end of a passage that
teaches us about the mercies and blessings of God and how these
are combined with his punishments. It is important that we suit
our discipline, both the rewarding and punishing aspects, to the
individual child. Each child is different. What is proper for one is
too harsh for another. What works with one frustrates another.
What motivates one discourages another. This is particularly
important with children who are adopted and have experiences
different than they would have had if they had been in your home
from birth. How can you punish a child who has been previously
abused by beatings and cigarette burns on his back? Is there any
physical punishment that is likely to be effective and suitable,
given all that the child has endured in the past? How can you
motivate a child who has been constantly put down and ridiculed?
While we cannot always answer all these kinds of questions, they
are important. God deals with us in particular ways because ''he
knows our frame.'' He knows what makes us tick!

Ginger was a child very difficult to discipline. She seemed to
come and go in her own private world. No word from an adult
penetrated her world unless it was in agreement with her course.
In exasperation, her adopting parents turned to spanking and
discovered that pain would break into that private world. Following an angry spanking, she would be docile and loving for a little
while. The spanking increased because it seemed to work—until
the parents realized this was the pattern that had previously
accelerated to a point of child abuse and termination of parental
rights. It was the way Ginger had originally learned to relate to

adults and she was reacting to her new parents in the only way she knew. They had to find a new way together. When we deal with our children, it should be with a similar concern for individuality.

As we consider particular situations throughout the book, we will have further suggestions about discipline that emphasize God's model.

God is a parent who gives us freedom and holds us accountable. We have said that one purpose of discipline is growth, a major goal of all parenting. As we grow, it is necessary that we learn how to handle freedom and that we develop a sense of accountability before the Lord. It is difficult to watch our children make wrong choices and suffer the consequences, but parents must often go through the agony. God has allowed us to make choices, and some of those choices are real disasters. Beginning with Adam and Eve, we have been faced with freedom and accountability. Christ said, "Ye shall know the truth, and the truth shall make you free . . . . If the Son therefore shall make you free, ye shall be free indeed" (John 8:32, 36). This freedom in the Lord allows us to make choices, it allows us to grow, and it cultivates accountability. Some of the parables of Christ teach us that if we do not use those gifts that God gives us, we will lose them (Matt. 25:29). Throughout the Bible there is a principle: "use or lose." If we do not teach our children to use freedom, they will lose the ability to make adequate choices and to take responsibility for their actions.

Teenaged Shana and her mother argued for two weeks about a new coat. Shana wanted one styled in the latest fad and color. Her mother insisted that since a coat was a basic garment she should plan to wear at least two years, it should be a classic style and color. Finally Mother agreed to Shana's choice, stipulating only that the coat would be the only one purchased for two years— whether lost, accidentally ruined or just disliked as out of style. Long before the two years were up, Shana admitted her mistake. But allowing her to make a choice and holding her accountable for it also permitted her to learn how to budget more wisely for clothing. Many choices will be less significant, many far more important, than a coat style.

God is a parent who is patient and enduring. God takes a lifetime
to build in us the characteristics of his beloved Son. As we grow,
God shows himself to be a patient and enduring parent. Christ
agonized over Jerusalem (Matt. 23:37–38). God called to the
children of Israel with both anger and anguish in his heart. He is
pictured as being "merciful and gracious, slow to anger, and
plenteous in mercy" (Ps. 103:8). The Bible speaks of a God of
changeless love. Because of his enduring patience we are spared
(Mal. 3:6).

Parenting takes both patience and endurance. Children grow
up, but that process may be a difficult and even agonizing one. In
all cases it is a journey of faith for parents and children. Christians
usually come to understand that salvation is of the Lord and not
by our own works of merit. But we sometimes have great difficulty
realizing that neither can our good works secure spiritual blessings for our children. The responsibilities of parents are immense
and are clearly pictured in Scripture, but we cannot place our
confidence for outcomes in our children's lives on our works.
We must depend on faith in the mercy of God toward us and
toward them.

Children grow slowly. They have many false starts and many
stumbles. If we are without patience, it is likely we will also be
without hope. Paul tells us that it is through patience and comfort
of the Scriptures we have hope (Rom. 15:4) In Hebrews we are
told to run with patience that race that is set before us (Heb. 12:1)
This counsel brings to mind the long-distance runner. That is a
good picture of a parent. Parenting is a prolonged race that takes
patience and endurance. But just as many have found exhilara-
tion in marathon jogging and long-distance running, we can find
the endurance of parenting to be joyful rather than drudgery.
Christ encourages us so that we might be "strengthened with all
might, according to his glorious power, unto all patience . . ."
(Col. 1:11).

Not long ago a young man joined our small-group Bible study.
The discussion that evening centered in the life of Jacob and the
patience of God in dealing with him over many years. Most of the

group was moved to tears as the young man told us about his years of rebellion in his adoptive parents' home. Seven years since leaving home and wandering like a prodigal, he had participated in the Lord's Supper just the day before the Bible-study meeting. He was now rejoicing in the patience of his parents and of God in waiting for him to come to know the Lord and to come home.

God is a parent who sustains us by providing and withholding. Like our children, we often make wrong choices because of our material desires. Because we worry about having enough, our freedom is turned against us. Although we know that God is Father of all mercies and God of all comforts, we still worry that our needs will not be provided. We also long for many things that are rightly classified as "wants" rather than "needs"! God deals with us as a generous parent, but he also withholds what will not be good for us. When Jesus said ". . . your heavenly Father knoweth that ye have need of all these things" (Matt. 6:32), he was talking about food and drink and clothing and a place to live. But we still have struggles. Just as our children frequently want things that we can see will not be good for them, we want things that God knows will not be good for us. In God's loving provision and wise withholding, we have a model for our behavior as parents. Loving means giving. But loving also means withholding those things that are not good for us. God gives us this encouraging promise: "Delight thyself also in the LORD: and he shall give thee the desires of thine heart" (Ps. 37:4) Not only does God give us good things and withhold bad things, but he also promises to change the desires of our heart so that these very desires are those given by him. As we deal with our children we will meet innumerable occasions when they will say, "I want." God's model shows that we should both provide what is necessary and good and withhold what will not be good or profitable for them. Sometimes the proper answer to "I want. . ." is "No!"

God is a parent who is forgiving and full of mercy. "He hath not dealt with us after our sins; nor rewarded us according to our iniquities" (Ps. 103:10). There is a principle of Scripture that says we *don't* get what we deserve, and that should be a great encouragement to us. Although we reap much of what we sow, none of us gets totally what our sins would deserve, because God is merciful and gracious. He pities us as a father. Jesus told the parable of the prodigal son (Luke 15:11–32) to illustrate the mercy and forgiveness of God. We all make mistakes. We all break the commands of God. We all leave things undone we should have done. We all reject part of the good that God has stored up for us. In spite of this, God shows us mercy and forgiveness and invites us back into his household. For his behavior, the prodigal son had feasted with the pigs at his banquet-of-consequences. There was nothing that could give him back the time and resources he had wasted, but the future could be changed and *was* changed by his loving and merciful father. As we consider our children we will find that they are sinners. They will do things we don't like and don't want, and all will have sparks of rebellion. Some of these sparks will be doused and some will be cultivated into full-blown fires. The joys of parenting will be tempered with the anguish of sin. But joy can be restored by forgiveness and mercy. Paul listed the gifts given to Christians in Romans 12. It encourages us that he exhorted: "...he that showeth mercy, with cheerfulness" (v. 8). That is exactly how God shows mercy to us. Cheerfully, joyfully, with much singing and rejoicing.

Yesterday one of our grown daughters took her ten-year-old cousin for a walk and a treat, and he returned her kindness with a mean little trick. She reproved him quietly, and he responded with no remorse and ran away to the television. After thinking for a bit about what would help him most, she went to him and said, "Joey, even if you aren't sorry, I forgive you for doing that mean trick. Shall we shake hands and not be mad?" He ran to her and said, "I am sorry—let's hug instead." Our forgiveness wholeheartedly given paves the way for restored relationships. The Bible tells us that the goodness of God leads men to repentance.

As we pattern ourselves after God the Father, let us show forgiveness and mercy to our children with cheerfulness so that the joys of the family may be constantly restored.

Children and the Adoption Triangle

"You must let little children come to me and you must never stop them. For the kingdom of God belongs to such as these" (Mark 10:14, *Phillips*). "Believe me...unless you change your whole outlook and become like little children you will never enter the kingdom of Heaven. It is the man who can be as humble as this little child who is greatest in the kingdom of Heaven. Anyone who welcomes one child...for my sake is welcoming me" (Matt. 18:3–5, *Phillips*).

Radical Perspective on Children
Jesus turned the world-view of his disciples upside down. Those who would be the greatest must become the least! Those who would be first must become last! These familiar words were astounding to the disciples, just as they astound us if we really hear them and check ourselves by them. We assume that a child's goal is to grow up quickly and become adultlike. Jesus says that the goal is to become childlike, even as an adult! We assume adults are more important than children, but Jesus reverses the priority.

This certainly was not the way the disciples regarded children. Their attempts to prevent children from bothering Jesus gave him the opportunity to teach them the role of children in the kingdom of heaven. In the eyes of the disciples, the children were an annoyance and certainly not important enough to take up the busy time of the Master Teacher. The common view of children in modern society retains these attitudes of the disciples, which Jesus corrected and reproved. Both Christians and non-Christians approach many situations from the standpoint of the needs, desires, power, and influence of the adults involved. The desires and needs of children are regarded as annoying or unimportant or at best of secondary importance.

A biblical view of adoption requires us to shift our attitudes and align them with the teaching of the Lord Jesus. We must see the unique position children occupy in the eyes of God, who has placed children—and adults who need help in supporting children—at the center of Christian faith at work in the world today. James tells us that true religion as opposed to lip service is tied into ministry to children. He says, "Religion that is pure and genuine in the sight of God the Father will show itself by such things as visiting orphans and widows in their distress . . ." (James 1:27, *Phillips*). God has given children high priority and position in his kingdom.

Children are a gift. While children are God's gift to us, it is also clear that we do not own them. Recognizing this in our relationship to them helps avoid un-Christian attitudes toward our children. They are not a product we have manufactured. They are not a tool we can shape for our own use. God gives us children, not to serve as a vehicle for our own self-expression or to accomplish our own ends, but in order that they may be nurtured, trained, and prepared for his service. An attitude that implies that "this is my child and I can do what I want with this child" is radically sinful. Only as our own desires are formed and directed by God's Holy Word and Spirit can we safely impose our human will in the rearing of a child.

Children are valuable in God's sight. Children are also a very valuable gift. Jesus himself came into the world as a baby and added the weight of his glory to the fact that human children are of inestimable value. Perhaps to further emphasize their value, Jesus went out of his way to use them in teaching his disciples. Environmentalists remind us of the pressure of overpopulation on the world's resources. Some feminists are concerned that the burden of child rearing wastes the talents and gifts of women. Employers seem to regret the distraction that parenting can be to the single-minded pursuit of a career. But the Bible does not undervalue children in this way. They are worth great cost to God.

Children are persons. Scripture also establishes the principle that children stand before God as individuals. The personhood of children is seen in Scripture in a number of ways. In Genesis God established that at the time of marriage children would leave their fathers and mothers and cleave to each other as husbands and wives. A child is not an appendage of his parents (or "*her* parents"—here and elsewhere we will use the simpler masculine form for pronouns, but always imply either gender) who will someday be cut off, but is an individual who will at some point leave by choice. Personhood of children is also seen in that they are given moral status in the womb. Psalms 51 and 139 in particular speak of David's sense of God's caring and his own accountability from before his birth. Job spoke of the fact that death can occur in the womb. He said that the dead child enters Sheol, the realm of the dead into which adult persons enter. As David mourned for the lost child born to Bathsheba, he said the child had gone to a place where he would eventually join him. Both Isaiah and Jeremiah speak of God's call upon their lives as coming while they were yet in the womb. Taken together, these Bible references indicate that the child from earliest days has standing before God as an individual person.

A Special Relationship

A child's standing before God as an individual person does not contradict the fact that God places children and parents in a special relationship to each other. This relationship is pictured in our relationship to God. We are the children of God. As God's parenting serves as a model for our parenting, our behavior as children of God serves as a model for our children's relationship to us. Jesus Christ, the Perfect Son, serves as the model for us and our children. We can look at Jesus to see what children are to be like in relationship to parents.

Jesus was obedient to the Father. Children are to obey parents. They are not to rebel. They are not to rise up against parents or try to be rulers. In fact, the prophets say tough times are to be expected when the Lord gives Israel children for princes (cf. Isa. 3:4–5; Ezek. 22:6–7). We do our children an injustice when we do not expect them to be obedient. It is important that we recognize that the child is an individual, but this recognition must come in an atmosphere where obedience is expected.

The atmosphere must also emphasize training that teaches accountability. In all things we are accountable to the Lord, and in various ways to each other. The child is in a position of accountability to parents. Jesus taught that his obedience was due to his

relationship to God the Father. His whole life was a testimony to
the fact that he delighted to do the will of the Father (Ps. 40:8;
John 4:34; 5:30;17). He taught the disciples that just as the Father
had sent Jesus the Son and had loved him, even so was he sending
his followers and loving them.

We cannot claim, as Jesus did, that we have perfectly kept the
will of the Father and that we have perfectly finished the work that
he has assigned to us, but the model of Jesus as an obedient Son
is the perfect example of loving obedience that we should model
for our children. If we are rebellious and disobedient toward God,
it will very likely be reflected in our children's attitudes toward us.

Jesus had a relationship of love with the Father. Sometimes we
are tempted to think that obedience and discipline are contrary to
love. But in the life of Jesus we see one who was perfectly
obedient and disciplined and yet simply abided in the love of the
Father. He said, "If ye keep my commandments, ye shall abide in
my love; even as I have kept my Father's commandments, and
abide in his love" (John 15:10). Obedience and love are not
opposites; they are intertwined. Jesus obeyed because of the love
shown to him. He enjoyed that love as it led him to obedience.

Our children should see that we obey the commandments of
God the Father because of the love that he has shown toward us.
We love him and keep his commandments *because* he first loved
us. We want our children to love us and obey us because we first
loved them. Obedience motivated by the parents' love is much
stronger than obedience motivated by fear of punishment.

Jesus trusted the Father for outcomes. When Jesus came to earth,
he accepted the limitations of being human. He temporarily laid
aside aspects of his equality with God and endured all types of
temptation, just as we do. One of our constant temptations is
worrying about outcomes. We worry about what is going to
happen tomorrow. We worry about what might happen when our
children hit the teenage years. We worry about worrying if we
have nothing else to worry about! Jesus also met that temptation
to worry, and he overcame it. He trusted his Father for the
outcomes. Even when he could not totally see what the outcomes
would be he trusted. Part of Jesus' struggle in the Garden of

Gethsemane was to lay down his anxieties and simply trust the Father to bring all things to pass. In an intellectual sense, God's children know that all things work together for good to those who love God, but living that knowledge is difficult. It also is difficult for our children to trust us as parents for the outcomes.

We can help our children learn to trust the Lord and to trust us as parents by showing that same type of trust in our heavenly Father. It might bring us up short to have a child say to us, "Daddy, you say things are going to come out all right because you trust God. So why are you worrying?" Such a question gets to the heart of the matter.

Our children should be able to see love, trust, and obedience in our relationship with God, our Father. This will be the model they need as they respond to us as parents.

While we start with the triangle of God-parents-child, what we hope to end up with is a family where the triangle is a cohesive body. We want our children to see in us those characteristics of the Lord Jesus Christ that will help them to become strong in the Lord. We desire our children to love us and to regard us with the love and respect and obedience that the Lord is building into our relationship with him. While the relationship and view that we have of parents and children are important, this perspective needs support and help that can only come from binding ourselves together in the Lord. A triangle is a useful but rather flat and lifeless way to look at adopting families. What we are building are growing, changing families, reflecting on earth as best they can the loving perfection of relationships in heaven. In this chapter we have discussed primarily the nature of God as it applies to adoption and the position of parents and children in the adoption relationship. Throughout the book we will come back to these basic ideas. In addition, as we write about particular situations and processes, other biblical teachings about the nature of men and women and boys and girls will be considered.

2

Why Adopt a Child?

Our older son originally came to live with our family as a foster child. We had begun caring for foster children because we had only one child and were told by our doctor that we should not expect further pregnancies. We wanted more children. So when our son reentered the foster-care system after a year away from us, we asked the agency to begin the process of adoption. We were warned that the proceedings would be time-consuming and possibly unsuccessful. Six months after his return we shared with his caseworker the unexpected news that Evelyn was pregnant. In the conversation that followed we were asked: "Do you still want to adopt?"

Some potential adopters find the whole process of having their personal motivations and capacities to adopt scrutinized by social workers or others a very disturbing practice. "After all," they reason, "no one asks biological parents whether they want a child or whether they can rear it. Why ask me?" In the section on agencies we will deal further with agency evaluation of adoption applicants. We believe the decision to adopt requires an extra measure of self-evaluation, which often can be assisted by others.

In the meantime, one of the best ways to prepare for interviews with adoption workers is to thoroughly examine your motivations, abilities, expectations, and reservations about adoption.

In this chapter we will present the most common reasons for adoption. We will also discuss self-assessment ideas that will help you bring your family motivations and capacities to adopt under the scrutiny of God's Word and Spirit. In chapter 3 you will find information about the general adoption climate, agencies, and independent adoption. Chapter 4 will present information about matching available children and parents. From studying these three chapters we hope you will reach clarity of purpose and direction as you learn more about yourself and your family and about the myths and realities of adoption today. As you consider this information, pray for self-understanding and insight from the Holy Spirit who knows our hearts and directs our plans.

Motivations to Adopt

Motivations to adopt are diverse and usually reflect the individual circumstances of the adopting parents. There are a number of factors that lead couples to want to adopt one or more children.

Infertility

A generation ago the majority of all formal adoptions in the United States took place because the adopting couple was unable to have children born to them. Adoption was commonly suggested as a solution to infertility, as the question we were asked implied. If you can give birth, would you adopt? In our case the answer was yes, because we no longer thought of adoption as an answer to infertility, but as a way of making a particular little boy part of our family. But many couples are infertile, and for them adoption may be the solution for their childless state.

Approximately 15 percent of all married American couples of childbearing age are infertile. This translates into four to five million couples. For roughly a third of these it is the wife who is infertile; in another third the reasons for infertility lie with the husband. In the remainder of these cases some combination of factors appears to be at work. Infertility appears to be on the increase, for any number of suggested reasons including the possibility of better reporting of such statistics today. One important factor appears to be the delay of childbearing that is taking place among couples, which is known to increase the likelihood of difficulty in conception and bringing a pregnancy to term.

The percentage of apparently infertile couples who can be helped to achieve pregnancy is also rising. About half of them can achieve a healthy childbirth when the most up-to-date treatment is available and used.

This book will not include a comprehensive discussion of the methods of treating infertility problems, since such information is readily available. As in every other field, there are both competent and less-competent professionals, and the best protection against spending a great deal of money and time in a futile search for help is to become self-informed about fertility treatment options. Some suggested reading material is listed in the bibliography. In addition, Christian couples will want fertility counselors who understand their religious views and can help them find solutions within their conscience. *In utero* transplants, artificial insemination, surrogate wombs, and certain other fertility solutions have moral dimensions. Some specialists are not equipped to deal with these and may provide technique and treatment in what amounts to a moral vacuum. The burden for assessing the moral implications of various fertility procedures may rest solely on the couple. On the other hand, if you raise the issue, it is possible that the doctor may be quite able and willing to discuss the procedures in these terms or can refer you to a colleague who will.

Roughly 50 percent of childless couples will not find a solution to infertility, no matter how vigorously pursued, and others will decide that the expense, frustration, and/or morality of some possible attempts to achieve pregnancy are not for them. At some point in this process of dealing with infertility, some person is very apt to say to that couple, "Why don't you just adopt?"

Usually the question is well meant, but it overlooks a very important truth. Adoption is not the immediate response to being unable to have a child. Grief is the response that most people feel when confronted with news that they will be unable to have the children they expected. Before couples can go on to planning a different future for themselves—which may or may not include adopting children—they need time to come to terms with their lack of childbearing capacity. They need time to grieve and recover. Jumping into adoption makes no more sense than re-marrying on the way home from the funeral of a spouse, and it may carry the same kind of problems for parents and children that quickie second marriages bring.

Grieving for this loss is complicated by the fact that it is a very private affair. Sometimes the couples cannot share their disappointment with each other, fearing the spouse will feel blamed or angry or cheated in some way. Frequently those feelings are present and, if so, it will take courage to face them and discuss and resolve them. Other members of the family are also involved in this disappointment and may make the burden worse by thoughtless comments and repeated inquiries as to when children may be expected. Even casual acquaintances sometimes feel free to question childless couples, and the couple is left with the dubious choice of revealing a painful secret or accepting an undeserved reproof. One couple stopped going to baby showers because the remarks directed to them were so thoughtlessly unkind.

Many couples have found that it helps to share their particular sense of loss in a small group of other couples who are also infertile. Sometimes adoption agencies are able to suggest a suitable group, or your pastor may know of other couples in the congregation who have worked their way through infertility grief and can help you. The small amount of literature on the subject seems to suggest that a process similar to other grieving takes place, with anger, bargaining, depression, and acceptance all factors that gradually yield place to healing. In this process it is important to remind ourselves that God sees this hurt as he sees all others, that he hurts with us and will provide the healing.

When the couple has come to terms with the infertility, has grieved for this loss and accepted it, they will then be ready to consider adoption, taking into account the same kinds of factors other couples who adopt must consider.

Altruism

Some couples first begin to consider adopting a child because they want to find a way to express their urge to do some good in the world, in particular some good to help children. This motivation takes various forms, and a Christian couple needs to examine the assumption that what they want to do is in fact "good." To do that, they need to examine the facts of the situation and the results that may be expected from using adoption in the situation. Later in this chapter we will provide some information to assist you in examining altruistic adoption today.

There is a widespread feeling that the world is becoming overpopulated. In many sections of the world people are starving. Because our consuming society puts great pressure on natural resources, some Christians have decided that rather than have additional children, or even one child, they should adopt those already born. By doing so they relieve population pressures to that degree.

Another group of potential adopting parents hopes to bridge cross-cultural gaps and promote international or racial brotherhood by adopting across national or racial lines. Once widespread, this practice has come under scrutiny from a number of quarters. In particular, the Black Social Workers Conference and various overseas governments have moved to try to slow the adoption of children outside their ethnic heritage. The current argument in this area will also be presented for your consideration.

When we asked couples why they decided to adopt, many answered quite simply, "We wanted to give a child a Christian home." Certainly that is a good reason to consider adoption. You need to know that in child welfare, as in every other field, there are fads and fashions. Any expressed motivation that suggests the person may be trying to rescue another person is now highly suspect in many agencies. For reasons that are not quite clear to us, "rescuing children" by adoption is now a negative idea almost equivalent to "child snatching." The general public, professional literature, and government programs are heavily geared toward keeping biological families together and the theme is "support the family." In many circles there is a definite bias against adoption. There are still children who need "a Christian home," but do not be surprised if the agency you visit does not warmly welcome your offer. They may be more impressed by other motivations. But hang on to that desire—it will help carry you through some days when self-centered reasons would not be adequate to carry out a difficult adoption.

A Way to Complete a Family

Quite often, couples who could have any number of biological children plan, even as early as courtship days, to adopt some of their family. They see adoption as a desirable way to build a family, just on its own merits. In many such cases one (or both) of these adults is adopted or has siblings or other relatives who were highly successful adoptees. Many agencies are looking for such families. While research is unclear to support the idea, there is a feeling that couples who already have biological children may be more relaxed and accepting of individual differences in children and able to cope with difficulties in child rearing. If you are willing to accept a hard-to-place child, the fact that you already have children will likely be regarded as a plus. This is a change in practice and usually does not apply in the case of babies. Agencies still tend to place healthy infants with childless couples, partly due to the scarcity of babies available for adoption.

Love of Children

In addition to the couples who see adoption as a way of doing good in the world in general, there is a group of adults motivated to adopt by an intense love of children. They make room in their lives for children because they like being around them and watching a child develop. Very often, handicapped children have a special place in their love, as do children who for various other reasons cannot easily find an adoptive home. These families may grow by leaps and bounds, and outsiders sometimes wonder,

"Why do they do it?" If you feel you have that kind of intense love for children and would like to adopt for that reason, it is wise to spend a good bit of time working with children in other settings before you make an adoption decision. Perhaps you can volunteer at a handicapped center, tutor in a remedial program, or become a foster family. To borrow a popular book title, *Love Is Not Enough*. Many of the children available for adoption require tremendous strength in the adopting family. Years of giving with little emotional return and physically taxing labor are frequently required. Sentimental "love of children" will be inadequate. Mature love, undergirded by the love of God and combined with knowledgeable commitment, will be required. If you are adopting because you love kids, be sure you know what loving kids is all about. Another couple we know decided to adopt because "we just love babies." Obviously, babies—like kittens—grow up, and that adoptive mother confessed that she never really thought about the years beyond diapers. Although many babies are conceived and grow up in families without consideration by their parents of the long-term commitment, you have an opportunity in adoption to make a more thoughtful choice. Has God given you a love for children that motivates you to a steadily deepening commitment to the work of child rearing?

Provide for a Particular Child

Occasionally couples who never really thought much about adoption begin to consider this alternative because of a relationship with a particular child. Perhaps a relative, foster child, or student in your local school is personally known to you, and your family wonders about taking the initiative to seek adoption for the child into your family. Before deciding or committing yourself to the child, be sure to get some counsel from other Christians equipped to help. Some children who are quite content to live in your home do not react well to cutting all legal ties with their biological family. Alternatives such as guardianship sometimes can be arranged to provide stability without severance of all parental ties. Once again, sympathy or sentimental "feeling sorry" for the child is an inadequate motivation for adoption. Pity quite easily becomes hostility if the object of your care does not seem grateful—and many older children are not at all pleased to be adopted. They may continue for many years to want what they see other children have—their own biological families.

After reading this far, you may feel that we are very hard on parents who have good intentions to adopt. We do not mean to be! We are very positive about adoption and believe that it is God's perfect choice for many parents and children. But we do want you to think through your reasons carefully, so that you can communicate them to each other and to the persons who consider your application to adopt. In addition, some day your child will say to you, "Why did you adopt me?" What will you tell your child?

Bringing Motivations Under Self-Scrutiny

Having listed the reasons why couples may decide to adopt, we want to suggest a method for examining your own motivations and capacities. Probably you will decide that a number of your reasons for wanting to adopt blend together and that you have some strengths and some weak areas. You will have to decide if, all things considered, you are well motivated and have the potential for a successful adoption. The aspects we will ask you to consider are (1) applying the Word of God to your situation; (2) information about available children; (3) assessing yourself and your family.

The Word of God

All of us have heard stories or perhaps know at least one person who used the Word of God in odd ways while looking for direction. Perhaps the method involved opening the Bible and "discovering" personal instructions in the first verse noticed. We do not recommend that method! God has promised to direct us but not in superstitious ways. He says, "In all thy ways acknowledge him, and he shall direct thy paths" (Prov. 3:6) Certainly that applies to adoption. Hebrews instructs us: "For the word of God is living and active, sharper than any two-edged sword, piercing to the division of soul and spirit, of joints and marrow, and discerning the thoughts and intentions of the heart'' (Heb. 4:12, RSV). Jesus promised that he would send the Spirit to guide us into truth, and the context makes clear that part of this truth has to do with knowing ourselves. But how do we use the Word of God in self-examination of our situation and motivations?

Christians use various ways to seek the counsel of the Word of God, and you will need to choose what is best for you. When we have a difficult decision to make, we usually make it a matter of study, both privately and together for many days. In our quiet time we continue with whatever Scripture we have been using and ask God to direct our attention to any part that may have bearing on our particular situation. We listen for Scripture in public preaching that applies to the ordinary course of our lives. We do not expect bulletins from the sky, but direction from the ordinary use of the Word of God. Other Christians have found it helpful to go away for a weekend retreat devoted to examining a decision in the light of the Word of God, and they may choose particular passages to study or ask other Christians to suggest passages. Reading and study of the Word of God should be accompanied by prayer asking the presence and direction of the Spirit. We must also come to God with truly open minds, willing to have him tell us what we may not want to hear. God linked willingness to *do* the will of God with ability to *know* it. If we are not presently living obediently, or do not intend to obey, he has not promised us further guidance about his will.

What Kind of Children Need Adoption?

In order to examine your motivations to adopt, you also need good information. No matter how pure your intentions, if your actions are not based on accurate knowledge of the situation, you can mislead yourselves. In chapter 3 we will suggest ways you can get information you need, and chapter 4 will provide important information about the children who are waiting for families. Over and over again, adopting families have told us: ''If we had known more about the children, I think we would still have adopted, but we would have known more what to expect and how to get ready."

If you plan to adopt a "special needs" child, foreign-born child or one of a racial background different from your own, an older child, or a sibling group, you need specific information about these children and the controversies and difficulties surrounding their circumstances. You need to know what extra demands such children place on a family. Since such detailed information is beyond the scope of this book, we have added suggested reading material in the bibliography.

Assessing Your Family

Another part of deciding whether you should adopt has to do with getting to know yourself and your family. The better you understand what your family is like and how it works, the better equipped you will be to know whether adoption in general is a good plan for you and whether a particular child would fit into your family.

There are many ways of looking at families. We are going to suggest some ways you can examine yours. It is important to remember that there is no one ideal family that you must somehow measure up to in order to be considered fit to adopt. A wide variety of children need homes, and your family, which is different from all other families, may be just the one for a particular child. Many people with experience in past adoption practice feel that agency workers have been too ready to determine in their minds or policies that there are certain ideal families. They made lists of desirable characteristics, and these often had to do with such externals as age, marital status, income, home ownership, and church attendance. Applicants who did not fit the agency ideal were denied. Although it is hard to determine the degree to which such standards still prevail, it is clear that success as an adoptive family cannot be predicted simply by meeting these agency qualifications. In the past, independent adoptions on the whole appear to have been as successful as those arranged by agencies.

Recognizing the limitations of their previous policies, and under pressure from adoptive-parent groups and others, many agencies have tried to broaden their assessment policies. Families that once would have been automatically rejected are now accepted, and families that need help to become ready to adopt are given advisory services. In the rush to be broad-minded, some agencies have almost abandoned strict standards and decide on a case-by-case basis whether a particular family can successfully adopt a particular child. The majority of agencies have attempted to reach a middle ground. They tend to emphasize such parental characteristics as ability to arbitrate, to live non-isolated lives, to be tolerant, to be resilient. Ability to get along with the agency personnel continues to have a priority position in these characteristics desired by agencies.

In the absence of specific rules, agencies have tended to rely more on psychological portraits, such as ratings of emotional readiness, stability, and security to determine fitness for adoption. Whether or not in the long run this is more accurate than earlier measures, it is certain that the process is highly subjective and subject to worker bias. What one person calls ''tolerant'' another person may call ''wishy-washy.'' However, if you plan to use an agency, you need to be prepared for the kinds of interviews that will take place. You should be aware of the characteristics being sought, not so you can fake them, but so that you can accurately portray yourself. If you plan an independent adoption, there may not be anyone to help you evaluate your family and prepare for this life-changing event. In either case, time and effort spent learning what your family is like and how it works will be well spent.

The Process of Assessing Yourself

The following section will present three ways of looking at your family. We suggest that you do this assessment during a time when you and your spouse can work on it together. If you have children, they can be included at least part of the time, and this will provide many opportunities to prepare them for the adoption of another family member. You may want to do one part, then let the ideas simmer for a few days before reviewing and going on to the next section.

This is the outline we will follow:

1. Your family and the world—sources of support, strain, conflict and gratification.
2. The history of your family.
3. How your family works—boundaries, roles, communication and change.

Your Family and the World

Whether you are a single person seeking to adopt, a family of five with a desire for additional children, or a childless couple hoping for a baby, you need to consider how you fit into the world. What are your sources of support, what strains exist in your relationships with others, where are the areas of conflict, what gratifications are available to you? All of these have relevance to adoption, and, you are the person who can identify them. You will need a large piece of paper (a pad of chart-size newsprint works fine) and a couple of Flair-type pens.

Begin by listing across the top of the paper all the ways in which your family makes contact with the world. Here is a partial list to get you started: Work, Church, Recreation, Health Care, Social Services, Neighbors, Extended Family, Retail Shops, etc. You will think of additional contacts as you begin to work with your list. Down the left-hand side of the paper write Support, Strains, Conflicts, Gratifications. (See table.) Then consider your list of contacts one step at a time:

Supports. Begin with "work" and look at it first as a source of support. Be as specific as possible and list all the different kinds of job-related support you are getting. For example, in addition to money, there may be travel opportunities, or positive job relationships that help you cope with less-satisfactory relationships in other areas. Think about how each of these aspects of support would be affected by adoption. Go through your whole list, making notes or symbols to remind yourself of support aspects of each category.

Table 1 Our Family and the World

	Work	Neighbors	Church	Retail Shops	Social Services	Health Care	Schools Recreation etc.
Support	Money. Friends own age (Mother).	Trade-offs for house watching, etc. Emergency help.	Shared faith. Friendships with similar goals.	Handy and good prices.	Not yet tried.	Good local physicians. Small hospitals.	
Strains	Regular overtime cutting into Sat. chores (Dad). Housework plus job duties (Mom).	Noisy dog!	Emphasis of present church leadership not your emphasis. Temporary affiliation.	Many not open evenings for family shopping.	No local offices in our suburb.	Specialists are 35 miles away, in nearest major town. Mom visits regularly for chronic emphysema.	
Conflicts	Is it a job or a career? (Mother). Competition for a promotion coming up (Dad).	Too busy for real friendship	None at present.	Dad dislikes errand running but *can* do some on his lunch hour easier than Mom.	Is it "welfare?" (Dad).	None at present.	
Gratifications	Sense of satisfaction (Dad).	Security	Encouragement. Comfort.	Shopping is a pleasant evening out for Mom.	"Guess it's there if we need it."		

Strains. The next step is to consider strains in all these relationships listed. Examples of work strains might be uncertainty about a layoff, difficulty with adequate child-care arrangements, or overtime during certain seasons. What additional strains will an adoption place on relationships within each of these areas? Make notes as you go. You may also want to ask yourself: "Am I counting on the adoption to ease any of these strains? Is this realistic? Is this the best way to deal with this strain?"

Conflicts. Areas of conflict exist in our relationships with the world. In an ideal world such conflict would be met and resolved but this does not often happen. In the work area, for example, a person may feel he has no choice but to continue a job where he is experiencing a lot of conflict with a co-worker. Or there may be conflict inside the family over the extent of a family member's involvement with a job. Try to list areas of conflict or disagreement in this step without being distracted by conflict over your conflict! Once again, jot down any thoughts you have about adoption and the conflict area. For example, would there be conflict with your extended family over a decision to adopt an international child?

Gratifications. The last area to consider overlaps somewhat with support, and you may find you have covered this already. However, go back over your list again, since gratifications tend to be less concretely measured and you may gain new perspectives. Which of these sources of gratification will be lost if you decide to adopt? Which will be enhanced? Are some family members receiving many sources of gratification, while others have few or none? Would the adoption be regarded as a source of potential gratification by all members of the family? Do some stand to lose and some to gain?

Discussing your family together in this way may be quite new and difficult for you. When a family member seems hesitant to participate or bothered by what surfaces, try to encourage sharing without forcing. Accept what a person says without such statements as: "You shouldn't say that," or "I don't think you should feel that way." The point of the exercise is to understand what is happening in your family in relation to the world.

If whatever family members volunteer is judged in a negative way, they will stop sharing, and the process of arriving at the information will be short-circuited. You can squelch people's expressions of their feelings and opinions, but that does not make them go away—they may just go underground and become harder to deal with.

After you have filled out your lists of relationships, post it someplace where all the family members can look at it and think about it. When you get together to talk about the next aspect of your family, be sure to allow time to talk about any further ideas about your family's relationship to the world and how adoption would affect it. Be sure to save your chart.

The History of Your Family

After you have looked at your family as it exists in relationship to its environment, you are ready to look at your family as it has developed through time. Marriage brings together two adults who begin a new family. It is helpful to look at the family history of both adults in order to understand and appreciate the family the way it now exists.

Take another sheet of newsprint and begin to chart your family tree. Leave plenty of space for notes. It may help to use a circle to indicate females and squares for males. As you fill out the genealogy, note names, deaths, ages, occupations, and any other information that comes to mind. As you work at this, some patterns may emerge, and you may share some information with each other that has not come up before. "I didn't know you had a sister who died when you were nine." "Your grandmother worked in an office after she married. That must have been rather unusual in her day." "You know, it looks like we are a family of teachers and preachers. What would we do if our adopted child preferred truck driving?" "That name has been used for a boy for four generations. Guess it's up to us for this generation." The discussion of the family tree should flow freely. The object is to understand what expectations and traditions may be placed upon an adopted child and consider whether these are realistic and fair. These questions recognize that an adopted child also has a family

history, and just as your own marriage has required the merging
of two family histories, adoption will require further blending.

If there are children in your family, you will usually find they
enjoy the family-tree project very much and will like hearing
stories about your families. The sense of continuity with the past
is precious to children. Post your family tree and continue to add
to it as you think about your family history and about the meaning
of adoption.

How Your Family Works

Now we would like you to look at how your family works. To
do that we want you to think about four concepts: Boundaries,
Roles, Communication, and Change. As before, try to relate each
of these areas to your investigation of adoption as a plan for
your family.

Boundaries. Family boundaries refers to the idea that every
family exists inside invisible walls. The walls around the family
may be very high and tight, so that outsiders never really penetrate the family circle. Even in-laws and their children may not be
regarded as real family members. A good way to test who is
inside and outside the family is to ask and answer the question,
"Which adults know about the family skeletons?" Insiders do,
outsiders do not! Blood lines are what count in tight families. In a
crisis, family members are expected to look to each other for
help, not to outside agencies. It is easy to see that adoption would
pose serious problems for a family with strict boundaries. Even
the child might not be accepted as family. At the other extreme
are families where boundaries are almost unknown. A teenager
could bring a friend home to eat and sleep for a month or two and
other family members would hardly notice. Everyone goes by
first names, and the fact that someone is a first cousin by marriage
or was the third wife of a brother would be unnoticed and unimportant. Again, adoption might pose serious problems, for the
boundaries are so vague that a child might have difficulty developing a sense of belonging and stability in his new family unit.

Of course, most families fall somewhere in between. The bulk
of families in the middle and toward both ends can successfully

adopt, but knowing where you fit helps make a sound adoption decision. A teenager who does not need a new family but a stable place to live and "leave his high-school yearbook" might fit best in a family with loose boundaries. A Down's Syndrome child might do best where boundaries are tight and family members agree to love and protect each other at any cost.

To get a sense of the kind of boundaries you have, here are some questions you could ask about your family and about other units of your extended families:

Is there a family member who makes sure that everyone understands who is related to whom and how? Is this important to other family members?

Who knows the family secrets?

How often do non-relatives eat meals or make overnight visits to your home?

Whom do you ask for advice?

Who can come in your door without knocking? Visit you without calling ahead?

Other questions will occur to you as you begin to assess this aspect of your family. They lead naturally into a discussion of another set of questions that are especially important in older-child adoption. There are boundaries *inside* families between individual members, as well as around family units. Some families allow almost no private space—opening each other's mail, going through drawers, and ignoring closed bedroom doors. Others are more like collections of individuals who happen to live under one roof with minimal interaction and support. Try to consider your family style with respect to personal boundaries and how an adopted child would fit into that style. Of course, the extremes again present the most difficulty, and the middle ground leaves room for adoption of children with various kinds of needs. If you know what your family is like, and the child's worker has correctly assessed the child's style, you should be able to decide if a satisfactory fit is possible.

Communication. You should also look at your family in terms of its communication system. Often those outside a family can determine very little about communication inside that family, but you can assess it for yourself. For example, most of us know at least one family where the mother seems to do most of the talking for her husband and children. Yet the fact that they have chosen her to speak with the outside world does not mean that they are unable to communicate quite clearly to her what they want her to tell the outside world. Here are some questions to ask about your family communication:

Are children allowed to express opinions or ideas?

Does one family member routinely speak for another?

Does verbal communication give the same message as non-verbal communication? (For example: She *says* she is listening but goes on reading a book.)

Do family members frequently say (or feel), "You're not listening"?

Who knows you are thinking about adoption? What do they think?

Do you arrive at decisions by talking, or does one family member usually just make them?

Do you usually solve problems satisfactorily by talking?

Overall, is your communication style working?

Adoption is a significant step that needs open discussion and communication ahead of action. In addition, you will need good communication to rear children with satisfaction and some measure of success.

Roles. Changing family roles have received so much media attention in the last decade that one would almost have to be a desert hermit not to be aware of the importance of the subject.

Adoption agencies have traditionally had a definite preference for families in which traditional husband-wife/parent-child roles were clear. Some now make an effort to avoid saying that certain ways of organizing family tasks seem to work better than others. Like the population in general, Christians vary widely in their opinion as to proper role division between the sexes and between parents and children. We, too, are unwilling to tell you how you must organize your family in order to be "biblical."

It is clear to us, however, that the role that family members agree to play remains quite stable. Such stability contributes to family well-being, and role confusion causes great difficulty when additional members are added to or subtracted from a family. Ask yourself these questions about roles in your family:

Are the roles clearly defined? For example: If "gardener" is the role of the oldest son, is he free to go about it in his own time and way? Or is it really still the father's role to be gardener-yardman, with only the specific task of cutting grass at a specific time delegated to the son? Or, if Mother is "laundress," does that role include gathering the dirty clothes and getting them back into drawers, or just seeing that the task is done?

Do people usually carry out their assigned roles? If father is "negotiator" with the outside world, does that include that unpleasant visit to the teacher, or will mother have to do that one?

Are members of the family generally satisfied with their roles? I (Evelyn) can remember expressing considerable dissatisfaction as a teenager (not necessarily justified) that I had the role of kitchen cleanup maid, while my sister had the compliment-generating role of dessert chef! Not only do families have task-related roles (breadwinner, cook, chauffeur, schoolgirl), they also have position roles. Who usually is the pacifier, the judge, the nurturer, the stand-in for parental authority (also known as top sergeant!), the clown, the whiner, the scapegoat, the brain? If there are just two of you, roles can be comparatively uncomplicated. Larger families almost unconsciously put people into multiple roles and keep them there. When additional children are added or subtracted, much tension may result until everyone shifts gears and adjusts to the change, whether loss or gain.

What roles will an adopted child be expected to fill in your family? Mother's companion? Father's fishing pal? A chip off the old block? A replacement to be nurtured instead of a child who died? Is the role expectation reasonable and fair? Does it fit the particular child?

Change. The family is a system. Like all systems, it must be able to adapt to changes over space and time. It is hard to assess your family's capacity for change before it happens, but we will try to help you see how you ordinarily deal with change and how you can strengthen that ability.

Seven years ago our family experienced enormous change, primarily because of accepting a new job. The house in which we had reared our family was sold, we left a close-knit, loving church relationship, broke our neighborhood, school, and community connections, made new living arrangements for the grandmother who formerly lived next door, and cut our professional ties. The shock of change was minimized somewhat by the fact that we knew the community to which we were going, had extended family and church acquaintances in the area, and would be near our young adult daughters. Emotionally, the most supportive factor was the conviction that we were moving into a new job situation at the definite call of God.

Three years later we moved again. This time the community was totally unknown to us, and we had neither family nor acquaintances nearby. We needed to find a place to live and a school for our high-school son, with no one to give us guidance. We had no church connections and no professional friends. We would be far from all our older children. This time the emotional support was principally that—so far as we could know—we were doing what had to be done and God would provide for us. But it took time for us to recover from the stress of so much change in so short a period of time.

Because we were foster parents for many years, with children entering and leaving our family unit, we have learned firsthand that change is always stressful. Some individuals can adapt more easily than others, and maturity helps one accept and deal with change. Since adopting a child will mean great changes in your family, ask yourselves these questions:

Do we plan to change? Or do we expect the child to change to fit our family system?

Are other major changes going to be taking place at the same time? (Adding a child is enough!)

How has our family handled change in the past?

Do all family members want this change and expect to adapt to it?

Can we handle a measure of discomfort and testing before things settle down again?

Is our family system flexible enough that people can accept changes in their roles at least temporarily while we fit this new person in?

Where do we expect difficulty? How will we handle it? (Specifically, list the changes you expect adding a child to make.)

Flexibility and the capacity to accept change in yourself and in your family is critical to successful adoption. Especially in the case of children older than infancy, character traits and learned patterns of dealing with a disrupted life may be very deeply imbedded. Where they are harmful to the child, you will want to help the child change, but this will take time. Meanwhile your flexibility will both model and make possible desirable changes in the child. Eventually both you and the child will be different and stronger than you were.

Every year thousands of infants and children are adopted by families in the United States. The emphasis by the agencies that serve them is on finding families for children, not children for families. Families similar to yours participate in the process. The possibilities for joy and satisfaction in building an adoptive family are tremendous. This chapter was written to help you consider your motivations to adopt and your capacities to parent the children waiting for families.

3

How Do I Go About Adopting?

Jim and Lois Bean spent their twenties in graduate school and getting started in careers. Now both thirty, they had recently decided to begin a family, only to learn that Jim is sterile. They have chosen to seek to adopt.

The Marsh family includes two children, Charlie (six), and June (three). Since courtship days, Mary and Tom had planned to complete a family of four children by adoption. They think the time has come to start looking for children.

Ted and Anne Smith are in their middle forties and have launched into adulthood the two girls they gave birth to early in their marriage. Anne is somewhat at loose ends and wondering about providing a home for an older child or two.

What should these people do next?

Getting Information

In chapter 2 we discussed motivations to adopt and family strengths and weaknesses. Now we will present information about adoption today. Some plans to adopt are based on false impressions or misleading ideas gained from the mass media, secondhand conversations, and emotionally based fund-raising appeals. Before deciding to adopt, you need to do a substantial amount of reliable information gathering. This chapter will help you go about getting information you need or would like to have. Good information is critically important to good adoptions.

Who knows about adoption? Who can I talk to? What do I need to know? Who has the information? What barriers to information are there? How do I get over and around them? These are important questions to those thinking about adoption.

Who Can Give You Information?

Libraries. People who are not in the habit of visiting libraries are often surprised at the wealth of knowledge available there and the helpfulness of library personnel in locating specific information. Good first steps in gathering adoption information are visits to college, church, and public libraries. In the back of this book is a reading list of books about adoption. Not all are equally valuable, so we have included a sentence or two to guide you into a particular subject or call attention to a point of view. If you live in a rural area with limited library facilities, it will take a little longer to get such books, but the local library will be able to borrow materials for you from state or other cooperating library systems. Try to read books from various points of view and keep an open mind to the viewpoints expressed. Some are quite shrill and challenging; some are a waste of time. You don't have to finish reading everything you start, but don't quit just because you don't like what you are reading! All of us need to learn some things we don't enjoy hearing. If an idea particularly strikes you, make a note of it and where you read it. You may want to go back and find it later or share it with someone else. After you have read several books about adoption, you will find it is hard to remember exactly what was said or who said it. If you have a reaction or question, add that to your notes for later thinking and discussion.

Other people. People who have adopted are a good source of information. Perhaps you are uncertain whether you should ask them about adoption, feeling they might regard it as invading their privacy. If the fact that their children are adopted is publicly known, it is unlikely that they will regard your questions as prying, especially when you tell them that you are interested in adoption and would like to talk to them about adoption facts. Very likely they will share facts and feelings about adoption. Among your acquaintances and friends who have adopted, there are likely to be one or two who try to recruit you for adoption! Aware of the needs of special children because of their own experience, they are always on the lookout for adoptive families. Be sure to listen, but do not make a premature decision because of their enthusiasm.

Adoptive support groups. As you look for information, you may stumble on or be directed to an adoptive-parents support group. You will be welcome as visitors, and we encourage you to attend. These parents can give you insight into the current adoption picture and a sense of the adoption experience after the ceremonies are over and real life goes on.

A number of adoptive parents have told us that they had talked to friends who had adopted or attended adoptive-parent groups, but that no one really told the truth about how tough or disappointing the experience might be. "Be honest with people," they said.

We suspect that learning how to listen to your sources of information may be very important. In our own experience, we have to admit that we did not really hear the warnings that were given. It may be true also that people did not always give the more pessimistic side of the picture. There are several reasons for this.

You may be discussing adoption with a parent who is finding much joy and satisfaction in the relationship with the child at present. Earlier fears, difficulties, and disappointments have been overshadowed by present good. Those difficulties don't come readily to mind. We were a foster family for many years, and there were hard, tiring, disappointing days and weeks. Some children we could not help. But when we discuss foster care with people now, we tend to remember and talk about the good experiences, which far outweighed the bad and brought us much happiness.

Some adoptive parents may not yet be ready to admit the difficulties in their family relationships. They are living on hope, or somehow believe that not acknowledging difficulties will make them go away. Although this is not very realistic, we all do it at times. If you talk to a variety of people, you will get a more accurate picture.

Some parents have not experienced the negative side of adoption. Since it really has been a smooth, easy experience, or at least well within the boundaries they expected, they see no need to comment on possible difficulties. Just as some biological children are easier to rear than others, some adoptions go more smoothly than others.

In this book we are trying to give you realistic information about what to expect. Your own experience may be much better or much worse than ours or others you talk to. In the final analysis, each of us must trust that God will provide the strength to live out the experiences he brings to us in adoption as in every other life event. Our role is to consciously move forward doing what we believe is God's will for us.

Adoption agencies. The third important source of information about adoption is the adoption agency. At this point it is not particularly important to know much about the agency itself. When you telephone the agency, tell them that you are just beginning to think about adoption and that you are gathering information. Ask if they can mail you some literature and see if they are holding adoption information meetings open to the public. Usually such meetings do not involve being an applicant for adoption. They are held to provide background information so that people can make a decision about whether they want to become applicants. If you already know what agency you plan to use, of course you will want to attend their sessions. Otherwise, any agency close enough for you to visit will be of some help in information gathering. You will have a dual purpose in attending this meeting. Take along a notebook and try to get a sense of the approach the agency takes to adoption as well as facts about children available, "suitable" applicants, and so on. Read the section on choosing an agency before you go, so that you can notice pertinent ideas. You are there partly to evaluate the agency, because this is one of the pieces of information you need to decide about adoption. You will be freer to ask questions and evaluate responses before you become an applicant. Some agencies, especially those that are national or international in scope, can be contacted for information by mail. There are addresses in the back of this book.

Professionals. Other specialized individuals can frequently give good information about adoption. Among the professionals you know, some may be knowledgeable about adoption. These include doctors, lawyers, ministers, social workers, guidance counselors, and many others. Any of these may be able to refer you to an adoption agency. We will discuss the role of individuals in independent adoptions later in the chapter. What you are looking for at this point is information and referrals to further information, not someone to handle your adoption. Do not make premature statements or commitments to any of these people. If any of them tries to push you faster than you are ready to go, be wary. Unfortunately there are unscrupulous individuals in every profession, and families seeking to adopt can unwittingly attract them.

Overcoming Information Barriers

Some couples and individuals find that there are barriers to overcome in seeking and getting the information they need to make good decisions. What are they—and how do you overcome them?

Out-of-date materials. You will spend only a few minutes in the library before you discover that much written material is outdated. Adoption is a rapidly changing field. Methods, children available, philosophies, public reaction, and even the purposes of adoption are changing. How will you know what is out of date? Look at the publishing date—it needs to be within the last decade, and the newer the better if you are trying to find out what the current situation is. This does not mean we think all the old theories are bad or that the new reality is always an improvement on the old. You will also find that much information does not seem to apply to your situation. To get around this barrier, try to adapt what is given so that it does have application to you. Or look for more material. There are many, many books.

Moving too fast. Another barrier to getting information is that people often want to jump to discussing you and your capacity for adoption while you are still trying to get the facts. You cannot know whether it is the right decision for you until you know what adoption demands. "Just the facts, ma'am" is not enough either, but it is the basic need. Try to keep focusing there, and make your questions as specific as possible. Write your questions down as they occur to you and take your notebook with you on information-gathering trips.

"**We know best.**" Adults gathering information about adoption sometimes run into a we-know-best attitude that is a barrier to getting information. This is most likely to happen in an agency that does not allow a participatory role for adoption applicants. Such agencies or individuals do not cooperate well in providing information, because they believe *they* have all the information to make a good decision on your behalf. Since you are the person responsible before God for the action you are taking in adopting a child, you cannot permit yourself to assume a nonparticipating role in the decision making. Since the first step is to have the information, you must find agencies or individuals who will share that information with you. Be frank, nonaccusatory, and non-defensive in making clear that you are an equal partner in this process, not a suppliant seeking the gift of a child. If you cannot get information you need in deciding to adopt through an agency, it is unlikely the agency will share information you need in deciding about a particular child. Your insistence may cause your application to be turned away by some agencies, but the establishment of honest communication with the agency is essential to a Christian process of adoption.

Reluctance to give information. We will mention one more information barrier here, although it will apply more directly later in the process. Some social workers are very reluctant to give information to you about a particular child, even after they have accepted your application and are suggesting that child for adoption by your family. This is a danger sign! Sometimes the agency has the mistaken notion that your willingness to adopt any child blindly is an evidence of the strength of your commitment to adoption. Your questions are then interpreted as uncertainty. This is a false assumption. Or they may be carrying the we-know-best attitude a step further—they do not believe you need the information.

In some cases, applicants may be cooperating in the silence about a child and his history, thinking that what they don't know they won't have to be responsible for sharing with the child later. Our position is that if you are going to make a child a permanent part of your family, all his history should be accessible to you, just as the history of a biological child is accessible. Sometimes the agency cannot share information because it does not have it. So far as possible, complete information should be gathered before adoption. Later attempts to seek information, even in the face of serious need, may be difficult, expensive, or impossible. The very effort to do so may put the adoption at risk. One parent wrote: "We'd like to give our adopted daughter some answers, but the agency is afraid that trying to get that information now will just bring the natural family back into her life at a bad time." Another parent said that she had been denied information about ethnic heritage. She added: "I wish I had been more assertive and pressed for an answer." Be cheerful, persistent, and firm. Parents need to know about their children.

On your part, be willing to listen to an experienced worker's cautions about sharing information with the child or any other person. Of course, the child may know some things you don't—a history of sexual abuse or fire setting, for examples. Such information should not be withheld from adopting parents, but occasionally it has been.

Types of Adoptions

You have looked at your motivations to adopt, assessed your family's parenting capacities, and read or listened to a reasonable amount of general information about adoption. Now you are ready for the next question: "Where should we go to arrange to get a child?"

Chapter 5 will deal with legal aspects of adoption in greater depth. Right now you need to determine who is permitted to serve as an adoption intermediary in your state. In about thirty states only agencies licensed by the state may place children for adoption. These are called agency adoptions. The agency may be either a privately run organization or a public agency supported by taxes. Some states also permit private adoption, which is also called independent adoption. In this method a private individual brings a child and adopting parents together, and the courts permit an adoption. Adoption is controlled at the state level and you need to know what is legal in your state. Any attempt to bypass procedures places the adoption at risk. Call a public agency to ask who may legitimately arrange adoptions in your state.

After you have determined the options, you will need to decide which method will be best for you. The advantages and disadvantages of each are quite clear.

Independent Adoptions

Independent adoptions are also known as "private," and "gray market." They are different from "black market" adoptions, which are arrangements that in some way violate the law, most commonly because of regulations having to do with excessive payments of money.

Advantages of independent adoptions. Independent adoptions tend to flourish in proportion to the length of time agencies ask adopters to wait for a child. A couple may be told that the wait for an infant is three to five years in an agency adoption, only to learn that a doctor friend knows of a baby available within weeks. Adoption itself is not a long process in most cases, so if you know someone who wants to give you a baby, an independent adoption has the advantage of speed. Other adopting parents choose independent adoption because they dislike the red tape of agency proceedings. It is true that some agencies and workers get bogged down in their own processes. However, it is well to remember that there is good reason behind most red tape. Do not jeopardize the adoption by failing to find a person who will scrupulously do all the necessary steps. On the other hand, many agencies are learning to cut some nonessential form filling and thereby streamline the processes. Independent adoptions are made with much less pre-adoption routine. You must decide whether you can safely avoid this.

Independent adoptions also hold the promise of flexibility. Humans manage to get themselves into situations that do not match the standard ways agencies operate. While some agencies can adapt to almost any situation, others cannot. Independent adoption offers an opportunity to tailor an adoption to the needs of biological family, adoptive family, and child. It permits an arrangement that is sensible and kind between the people directly involved. Many independent adoption arrangements have been made that adoption agencies would be reluctant to attempt. Some work out well, some not so well. If you are willing to take more risk than agencies recommend, independent adoption may work better for you. Of course, when adults take adoption risks, they are also placing children at risk. This fact carries with it substantial moral implications, and you must always consider the child's best interests. Adoptions that were once seen as "too risky" may later become standard agency practice when success has been demonstrated. If a child is already in care of an agency, the courts will seek the advice of the agency, and a strictly independent adoption will not be possible.

Independent adoptions are often arranged because they permit an openness that is not possible under the rules of some agencies. Confidentiality rules and privacy statutes may stand in the way of open-adoption arrangements. Some families are quite willing to permit contact with biological family, to promise regular letters or pictures, or to avoid in some other way the total break required in traditional adoption practice. Some parents who would not accept a total break are willing to relinquish a child for adoption on more open terms. Independent adoption offers individuals an opportunity to make agreements they can

live with. You should be aware that some agencies are also
arranging open adoptions and that often the safeguards to all
parties are more thoroughly thought out and practiced in agencies. Many agencies are also working for more general openness
in adoption practices.

Weaknesses of independent adoptions. The advantages of the
independent route to adoption are matched by some distinct
disadvantages. There *are* pitfalls to independent arrangements.

As a general rule, there are almost no services before and after
adoption in independently arranged placements. You will have to
make certain yourself that the child's biological parents are getting the counseling they need to make a good decision about the
welfare of their baby. Christians have a moral responsibility to
take seriously the fact that the child is arriving in another family.
You will also have to do the work of getting ready to be a parent
on your own. The fact that you have this book indicates you are
willing to undertake that work. After the adoption, you may want
to ask questions or discuss your feelings. There is some post-
adoption help available to independent adopters, but you will
have to find it on your own. Independent adoption places the
burden on you to be your own adoption agency. Do not minimize
or overlook the work that means you should be willing to do.

Independent adoption offers considerable opportunity for exploitation of all the parties involved. There is no national statute
under which unscrupulous persons involved in adoption rackets
can be prosecuted. Some hopeful adopters have spent quite a bit
of time and money without receiving a baby. You also may be
participating in a situation in which the biological mother is
exploited. You may receive a child that is not well or has congeni-
tal problems. Although these babies need homes, and you may
be quite willing to adopt such a child, you should know what you
are willing to accept and how you will handle such a situation.

A large national study of independent adoptions did not
find frequent cases of legal disruptions, but the investigators
did form the opinion that a proportion of independent adoptions were at risk if any party chose to exercise certain legal
rights. (Legal aspects are discussed in chapter 5.) The lawyer you

choose should have experience with adoption and be competent. Many adopting parents have their own private nightmares that "she'll change her mind and grab her child back." Agency adoptions have a better track record for protection of the adoption. Agencies attempt to be aware of changing adoption law and court decisions so that they can be honest about the legal risks involved.

Independent adoptions often do not provide follow-up resources. On the other hand, in most cases, it is possible to go back to an agency years later and learn medical facts, assist with a search for parents, or learn a family history. At least an agency is a starting point. Records for independent adoptions can be very difficult to trace, even when information is desperately needed.

In summary, independent adoptions have the potential to offer speed, simplicity, and flexibility. Their disadvantages are lack of service and risks to all parties and to the adoption itself.

Agency Adoptions

Now let us consider the advantages and disadvantages of agency adoption. Agency adoptions can be divided into those arranged by private agencies and those that are public, tax-supported services. We will consider public agencies first.

Advantages of public agencies. Public agencies are very sensitive to the fact that they may not use tax money and then discriminate against persons in illegal ways. For example, courts have warned agencies not to judge according to how obese an applicant may be, to avoid rigid age limits, not to favor a particular race, and so forth. It may be to your advantage to seek an agency where possible bias does not operate against you. Some private agencies are established to serve only certain clientele, and this is legitimate but may not include you.

Frequently a public agency has less expensive fees. In dollars this may mean the difference between a fairly nominal $500 fee and $5000 in a private agency. Some public-agency adoptions are handled without charge in case of financial need, or where the child being placed has been categorized "hard to place." Adoption subsidies are sometimes available to help with medical and other needs of children placed through public agencies. This may also be true in a private agency. As we mentioned, always ask about financial arrangements. If a public agency uses a sliding scale, you may end up with charges higher than a private or independent adoption would require. If you arrange an independent adoption and the court orders a home study, the agency may require a fairly substantial amount for this service.

Public agencies have access to a wide variety of children. Since it is very expensive to board and provide for children during a lengthy waiting period, many private agencies do not have the resources to handle exceptional children. If you would like to find a hard-to-place son or daughter, it is quite likely you will find your child in the waiting lists of a public agency. However, many private agencies cooperate with the National Adoption Resource Exchange and can help you locate children listed with this organization (address is in the appendix). Some private agencies also provide services to waiting children by arrangement with public agencies who purchase services from them.

Public agencies usually have good access to family support services. For example, the caseworkers there will know where you should take your adopted child for counseling help or remedial schooling. They use these services for children all the time and can help you find the people you need within your community. Often they can assist with paper work and interviews needed to secure services and may be able to arrange for reduced costs. Of course, a well-connected private agency will have similar services and resources.

Probably the most important reason people choose agencies (both public and private) are the advantages of having intermediaries in a very difficult human situation. Many people are involved; there are rights and responsibilities of varying intensity. It often helps to have an agency to stand permanently as either a facilitator of contact or a barrier. Occasionally we lose sight of the rights or needs of others as we become involved in our own wants. The agency (public or private) exists first of all to serve the needs of the child being adopted. Often that priority gives clarity and direction to a very complicated situation.

Weaknesses of public agencies. Public agencies do not have enough infants available to meet the demand. Given the present social and economic situation, that condition will probably continue. You may have to choose another source if you want an infant.

Because they do not have enough infants and they do have long lists of older and hard-to-place children, a public agency may try to push you into adopting a child who does not fit your family. Its workers are under severe pressure to place children in permanent families, and their need to get children into homes may conflict with your personal assessment of your capacities. It may be very hard for you to say "No," even though you have nagging doubts about a "Yes."

Public agencies are frequently seriously understaffed or staffed with persons with inadequate training and experience. If that is the situation in your community, it will be difficult for them to give you and the child adequate adoption services.

Some public adoption agencies are full of bureaucratic holdovers, in the form of either staff members or obsolete rules and procedures. Historically, public agencies are slow to change. You are somewhat more apt to run into a person or a procedure that makes no sense but is like a stone wall in the path to adoption. This is not to dispute the excellent work under trying circumstances that many public agencies are doing.

Some public agencies have a weak or inadequate philosophy of adoption, and others have a philosophy that is antagonistic to Christians. We will discuss this further when we consider how to choose a particular agency.

In addition to having some of the advantages and disadvantages listed for public agencies, private agencies have some that apply especially to them.

Advantages of private agencies. There is a tradition of excellence and pride in some private agencies that works to the advantage of their clients. Some have work standards that meet or excel any placed upon agencies by the courts or legislatures.

They generally have a strong commitment to the worth of adoption and strive to keep this option open to children and families.

Depending on many factors, some private agencies have resources not available to public agencies. Sometimes they can give more financial help to biological families, and this may help to bring prospective babies into their caseload. Usually the casework ratios are better, and a good private agency has some of the best adoption workers available anywhere.

Birth mothers who choose private rather than public agencies often mention the fact that they do not have to see themselves as welfare cases when they use a private agency and that the general attitude toward them and their situation is kinder and more helpful. In fairness to the public agencies, heavy caseloads and limited resources make matching this treatment difficult—it takes more than an attitude.

There is often more flexibility in a private agency. Innovations in adoption frequently come from this source, and you are more apt to win a hearing for an unusual proposal in a private agency. They answer to their own board of directors, not to every taxpayer in the state, and it makes risking failure a little easier.

In a private agency you are more likely to find an adoption worker with a compatible philosophy about life in general and adoption in particular. Private agencies represent a wide spectrum, and you need to choose one you have reason to think would understand you.

Weaknesses of private agencies. Private agencies may be quite expensive. Since they do not have tax dollars, they depend on endowments and private contributions. This often leaves a considerable gap to be filled by fees for services, and these higher fees may be a weakness of a private agency. Ask before deciding. Some private agencies are making conscious efforts to adjust their fees to be able to serve a wide range of people.

Private agencies may give priority to certain types of clients. For example, denominational agencies may give services only to members of their denomination. If you do not match that qualification, you probably can be referred to another agency and may find another private agency that prefers to serve people just like you.

To summarize, agencies offer comprehensive adoption service, provide safeguards and help to all parties, and serve a wide variety of children and families. Their potential disadvantages center around rigid procedures and shortage of healthy infants (particularly in the public agencies). Many of the parents who have adopted independently are well satisfied with their choice of method and feel that it was the best option for them at the time. Many others told us that an agency was a lifesaver in their situation.

If You Choose an Agency

Adoption is a life-changing step, and a good agency can provide invaluable support and help throughout the process. Unless you are quite knowledgeable about adoption, have a support system of other adoptive parents, or find yourself with no good choices in an agency, we recommend that Christians seek a Christian adoption agency.

Things to Look for in an Agency

As you begin your search for an agency, what should you look for?

1. *Licensing.* In most states, before an agency can accept children and seek adoptive families for them, the agency must pass license requirements regarding everything from the lighting in the parking lot to training of social workers. Licensing alone does not assure a good agency, but you should ask hard questions and get satisfactory answers before proceeding with an agency that does not have a license to operate in your own state. There are adoption scams that depend on the difficulty of interstate enforcement of license requirements.

For many years membership in the Child Welfare League of America has been important to establishing reliability in an agency. An agency may go beyond these standards, and not all

good agencies have joined the League, but it is one way to
determine an agency's standing. Many reputable agencies have
joined the National Committee for Adoption (NCFA). This organization has good standards for adoption practice.

2. *Stability.* Has the agency been in business long enough to
establish a good track record for handling adoption? Will it still be
around if you need help several years later?

3. *Professional competence.* Do they have trained adoption
workers, adequate and competent legal advice, enough staff to
give personal service, before, during, and after adoption?

4. *Access to support services.* Many of today's adoptions are
special-needs children, cross-racial placements, and older children. Can the agency arrange and follow through to get the help
needed by these children and their adoptive families? A dis-
appointed father said to me: "They handed me that little boy, and
I never saw any of them again. I think they just wanted someone
to pay his medical bills."

5. *Children to place.* Dismaying as it may sound, agencies are
now competing for children to place, especially white babies. You
need to know whether there is any reason to believe the agency
will have a child for your family within your time goals. Ask to see
figures on the number and ages and health conditions of children
they have placed in the last year or two. There are various reasons
why some agencies have more babies to place than others, one of
which may be an agency's willingness and ability to work with the
birth family in making choices for the baby. Some agencies also
have more money available to assist the birth mother with financial needs, though of course all payments must be legal. A
Christian social worker told me recently that "shopping for the
best deal" was becoming a problem even in Christian circles, and
it sometimes collided with choosing a Christian agency for the
birth mother.

6. *Financial arrangements.* Although costs will tell you very little
about the quality of the agency you are choosing, you need to
know about them. There are legal guidelines in most states to
prevent "baby buying," and agencies and adopters must scrupulously observe them or jeopardize the adoption. The charges

you pay will vary greatly from agency to agency. Some agencies operate on a fixed percentage of your annual income, some use a sliding scale, and some public and private agencies make no charge at all if you accept a hard-to-place child. Do not be afraid to ask questions about financial expectations. You should not be denied the opportunity to adopt because of finances, but your choices may be limited by them, and the agency knows you need this information. Reluctance to give it to you is not a good sign. A reputable agency will help you consider finances as one aspect of your decision to adopt.

7. *Philosophy of life.* One aspect of agency choice that you should consider seriously is its orientation toward Christians. It is easier to communicate honestly with an adoption worker whose philosophy of life is harmonious with yours. If the worker is going to help you effectively in the process of making adoption choices, it will be necessary to have a base of mutual understanding and respect that goes beyond mere surface politeness. If your worker disagrees with or minimizes the importance of Christian values, it will be necessary for both of you to act as though these did not exist in order to maintain the fiction of objectivity in the adoption work. *We do not recommend this approach.*

Many years of working in adoption have convinced us that there exists in many agencies a bias against Christians who take their profession of faith seriously in all aspects of their life. This is frequently expressed in adoption literature. The following attitude is not unusual:

> Agency requirements have until recently included restrictions that both adopters and caseworkers saw as too limiting, such as religion. . . . Researchers have discovered that some of the unhappiest adoptions are likely to be those by authoritarian parents with strict moral views, and that these attributes are highly correlated with the practice of religion, especially the fundamentalist Protestant varieties. . . . When adoption work is finally taken over by the state, the current argument goes, religious requirements and other bigotries of the private agencies will be ended. There will be no obstacle to the abolition of third-party placements,

because every one will be satisfactorily served by the agencies [*The Politics of Adoption*, Mary Kathleen Benet, New York: The Free Press, 1976, pp. 208–209].

No research studies are given in support of this statement about adoption outcomes in religious homes, although the publication includes a substantial bibliography in support of views expressed on other subjects. The writer's choice of words reflects her anti-religious bias.

The professional literature on adoption reflects little understanding as to why Christians and members of other religious groups consider the choice of religious orientation important. The transcendental quality of religion is often disregarded, and it is assumed that religion should be a matter of indifference to the biological family and the agency placing the child.

Certainly there are individuals working in public agencies who do not support this biased view, just as there are individuals in private agencies (even agencies labeled "Christian") who have little understanding of Christian values. We include this information to warn you that your definition of a good home for a child may include an element that some adoption workers find negative or unimportant. In searching for an agency, try to find out something about its actual philosophical positions.

Public agencies also operate in some states under anti-discrimination statutes with respect to age, marital status, and so on, which may operate in your favor. But these also limit the choices of biological mothers and fathers who may want to avoid certain kinds of placements. This is not primarily the adopters' concern, but it should be of concern to biological families and others attempting to choose an agency through which to place a child.

As in every other professional field, quality of adoption service varies. Choose the best you can find.

What Services Should You Expect?

If you have chosen to use an agency, what services should you expect? What will they want from you? If you have decided to be your own agency, what does that involve? There are three main stages to adoption—pre-adoption, the adoption itself, and post-adoption. An agency has particular functions to perform during each phase. You can expect the following pre-adoption services:

Information. Specific, accurate, detailed information communicated in a satisfactory way begins with the first contact. Most agencies today give a minimum of information on first contact, then invite you to attend a group meeting. The group meeting is usually spent outlining agency procedures, describing in a general way the children available for adoption, and answering questions. This session is sometimes used to weed out applicants by presenting a somewhat discouraging picture of adoption, especially infant adoption, in public agencies. Some agencies supply an abundance of information; others are more interested in finding out who is not a good candidate under their adoption requirements. Any questions you have should be answered if possible. It is reasonable to expect an adoption agency to provide the information you need about adoption.

Family assessment. At some point, the agency will move from information sharing to a process of assessing your family as an applicant. In many agencies this is called a home study. Another preferred term is "adopting family assessment." Home study or assessment procedures vary widely in thoroughness, how they are conducted, and attitude of those doing the assessment. A good assessment should help the prospective adopters know about adoption in general, understand their capacities to adopt, begin to correct weak areas, and give the adopter and social worker the information needed to plan a good placement. It is a shared endeavor between agency and clients. In the past adopters worried a great deal about the home study—with good reason. The object in many agencies was to permit a social worker to decide whether a family should be allowed to adopt a child. Many families did not pass, but most of them had little idea why they were rejected. Often it had more to do with children available in that agency than characteristics of the family.

Good agencies have tremendously modified their assessment practice to fit the goals above. How they proceed (individual interviews versus group meetings; home visits versus office visits, etc.) is less important than the prevailing attitude. The agency should communicate to you: "These people want to adopt a child. How can we help them do this?" Occasionally the decision to adopt may change during the assessment process, but it should not be accompanied by feelings of rejection as unfit to be parents.

Some agencies do the assessment and then ask the adopters to wait until a suitable placement can be made. Others first hold information sessions and do some preliminary work and then wait until near placement to complete the assessment. Completing an assessment and then waiting has the advantage that it readies a family in case a suitable child becomes unexpectedly available for placement.

Preparation for parenthood. Depending on your circumstances, you may want some specific pre-parenting experiences. Some adopting parents find it helps them feel more ready for adoption if they have a chance to talk to other parents, both prospective and present. This also helps develop a support group available to you when the child is placed. What Lamaze and La Leche are to expectant and nursing parents, adoption groups can be for you. If no such support is available, ask the agency to start a group or get your church to sponsor one. General parent-education classes are also good preparation for you. Agencies occasionally give parents the impression that mere willingness to attend many sessions regardless of family priorities and needs is proof of sincerity and commitment to adoption. If this happens to you, discuss the situation with your social worker.

Matching. At one time matching parents and children had to do with finding infants who were likely to grow up looking, acting, and performing as much like their adoptive parents as possible. Adoption was considered an attempt to create a family that could not be distinguished from a biological family. This concept of matching is dead and buried, for many good reasons. The kind of matching done now has little to do with genetic endowments and is meant to improve the opportunity to make adoption a success on its own, not as an imitation of birth families.

During pre-adoption the agency will be concentrating on getting to know you and your family. Good agencies also help you get to know yourself. Then they will present to you the children for whom they must find homes. The agency is responsible for knowing those children and communicating to you their characteristics, potentials, limitations, and prior experiences. You and the agency decide together what kind of children would fit into your family and how much you can change to fit a particular type of child. The process will become more and more specific until the agency has "matched" family and child.

That is how it is supposed to work! *Warning*: The placement process is sometimes shortcutted, haphazard, and just plain wrong. These are actual instances:

> A caseworker who had never met a family called to offer them a girl six months older than their first-grade son.
>
> A family from another county came to visit a four-year-old in foster care. The caseworker was not present for the visit, met the family briefly in her office, and sent the child home with them after a call to the foster parents telling them to pack the child's belongings immediately. There was no emergency involved.

If you suspect your pre-placement service is inadequate, *do not accept it* in your anxiety to have a child. Trust God, be patient, and do it right. Much pain and misery for all may be avoided. Ask questions like: "What have you seen in us that makes you think this child belongs in our family?" Or "What does this child want from parents? What is she used to?" Even average agencies are capable of giving good services when they are expected and used.

Pre-adoption and other parties. While serving you with pre-adoption work, the agency is also responsible for helping the biological family and specifically the child being adopted.

It is hard for you to know whether an agency has met the needs of the biological family, but this is very important. Their attitudes and behaviors will greatly influence the child, especially if beyond infancy. Not all situations can have happy resolutions for all the parties, but—if possible—the original family should have positive feelings about the adoption. As previously mentioned, Christian adoption is not child snatching but an intelligent, compassionate action to provide a permanent, loving family for a child whose own cannot or will not do so. The birth parents must be treated with respect and involved in the process as much as they are able, assuming, of course, that the agency is doing the necessary work to have legal basis for adoption.

The older child also needs preparation for adoption before you are presented to each other. Ask questions and get answers that make clear this has been done. Sometimes various subterfuges are practiced on children, and these invariably foster or increase distrust of adults. Any child beyond infancy can gain some idea of what is happening. For example:

> Becky was a foster child of four, living six months with our family, where she was very content. We had talked of the future from time to time, but Becky always insisted she would just stay with us. Finally the legal termination was secured, and her social worker came to talk to her about adoption and moving. She liked her social worker and had always asked her to visit again. That day as the social worker prepared to leave Becky was very quiet. As the door closed she called, "Don't come back. Don't ever come back." She understood a great deal and didn't like it much.

Children need time and help to absorb all the hurt and change that adoption means. They cannot anticipate the future until they have started to come to terms with the past. This work will begin in pre-adoption and continue intensively during placement interviews and visits. Do not try to hurry or take shortcuts. Child placement is a process, not an act. Sensitive, experienced casework now will minimize present hurt and make long-term success more likely.

Who Can Adopt?

In chapter 2 we discussed the kinds of qualities needed in adoptive families and suggested ways you could go about deciding whether yours is the kind of family that could adopt a child.

Outstanding among the characteristics needed are flexibility, realism, ability to work with others, stability, and caring and nurturing ability. They must be families with the inner resources to commit themselves for the long road involved in rearing children.

But we also told you that agencies no longer expect to be able to match perfect families and perfect children. We recognize instead that adults with varying combinations of strengths and weaknesses can be matched with children of widely varying needs and gifts to form successful adoptive families. Before you go on to your decision to adopt, you need to know more about the children awaiting adoption.

What Children Need Adoption?

Jenny is a newborn. Her teenage mother and father are not married, and they and their families have decided that Jenny should be placed for adoption as soon as possible and that her parents should continue in school. In the shorthand of American adoption, Jenny is a WASP—a white, Anglo-Saxon, Protestant baby whose mother received good prenatal care.

Todd is waiting in the hospital newborn nursery, too. No one officially knew that Todd was on the way until his teenage mother arrived at the emergency room of a large county hospital. Delivery was normal, but both mother and baby are now showing signs of drug withdrawal. No formal plans can be made because of the mother's condition, but she plans to leave the baby at the hospital. Adoption is a possibility. The child-welfare agency hopes to get sufficient information and consent before the mother disappears again.

Joel is eighteen months old and biracial. He was born with a cleft palate and has received corrective surgery, but additional operations will be needed as he grows. He is currently living in a black foster home with a sixty-year-old foster mother who loves him dearly.

Bobby, five; *Jimmy*, four; and *Donna*, eight, are also living in a foster family. Their present home is in a middle-class suburb, and there are two teenage children in the foster family. Their own parents were divorced just after Jimmy was born. The children have lived with both sets of grandparents, with their mother, and in foster homes at three different times. They have been in this home eight months, and their mother has now decided she cannot make a permanent home for her children and wants them placed for adoption. She has stipulated that she will consent, however, only on conditions that her children are placed together and she can see them from time to time.

Eric is a very angry nine-year-old Hispanic child. His teachers consider him incorrigible, and he has lived in three different foster homes in the past year. The latest placement seems to be going well, and his social worker and foster family are working together to prepare Eric for adoption. Eric's parents abandoned him to relatives when he was three, and he lived in a succession of relatives' homes. He came into the adoption network when an uncle delivered him to the agency after he attempted to set fire to their home. Eric has had a thorough pre-adoption assessment and is rated as bright, physically small but healthy. His history is so disjointed that it cannot be documented, but the psychologist believes some parent-figure abused him sexually.

Sue is thirteen. She has been in foster care with the same family since she was nine. Because everyone seemed satisfied with the situation, no one has made any push to clear her legal situation and secure an adoption. With the passage of foster-care review legislation, Sue's situation has come to the forefront, and her social worker is now seeking to make legally permanent arrangements for her. Her foster family has decided they are not willing to adopt Sue, in part because they feel her conduct toward them as a teenager has changed for the worse. They have also declined permanent guardianship and would prefer she be moved as soon as possible. Faced with this knowledge, Sue has become sullen and balky and insists she just wants to live in a group home and rejoin her natural mother as soon as she gets a chance. The agency wants to try to find an adoptive home.

Sherry is a severely handicapped infant. She spent the first two months of her life in intensive care and is currently living in a specially trained foster family. She is available for adoption, but if she survives infancy she will be a lifelong invalid requiring extensive medical care and much physical assistance at home. Specifics of her mental and physical prognosis are unclear.

Joe is a pleasant, overweight, mildly retarded fourteen-year-old boy, two years behind in school. He has been living in a large group home for three years but longs for his own family, especially a place where he can have a dog of his own. Joe has a grandmother who visits him from time to time and is fond of him, but she is in her seventies and physically unable to be responsible for Joe. It was she who brought him to the home and asked for help in managing him. Joe is black.

Aletha is four, and diagnosed as having intelligence above normal. She also has cerebral palsy and wears heavy braces on both legs. She attends an excellent center for physically handicapped children and has made great progress, but physical therapists expect that she will need intensive work throughout childhood and will be physically impaired as an adult. Her mother is not yet twenty, has had two additional children since Aletha's birth, and pays only sporadic attention to her daughter's progress. Aletha's mother agreed to foster placement because it became clear she was unable to take responsibility to cooperate with Aletha's treatment. She is not interested in reassuming care. Agency social workers believe she will give consent for adoption if the right family can be found. Aletha's parentage is unclear, but she appears to be multiracial.

All of the children described above represent actual children awaiting adoption. Homes have been found and successful adoptions arranged for children meeting such descriptions in the past. They are a cross section of the children in need of adoption today. In summary, the children are more often not infants; they frequently have mental, physical, or emotional handicaps; they come in sibling groups; they have had years of instability, poor parenting, or worse. Some of them long openly for adoption. Others have been rejected so many times that they are suspicious and hostile, no longer daring to believe there is a family to love them. These children often require huge emotional investments with no guarantee they can respond; their medical bills may be horrendous and their physical care a challenge to the health of the parents. Certainly, too, there are some healthy and normally intelligent infants or older boys and girls available for adoption. In addition, persistent would-be parents may be able to find a child in the international adoption network to join their family. These children may be born in another country and have all or none of the characteristics of the United States children listed above.

This may not be the adoption picture you had in mind, but it is reasonably accurate on a national level. The situation may be different in your local area, since the agency you seek may have more infants to place than are available as a nationwide statistic. There are severe handicaps and mild ones, emotional problems that respond quickly and those that leave deep scars. Some older children have had good homes until recently and bring healthy expectations and histories to their adoptive homes. Only thorough local checking will let you determine whether there is a child available whom God has planned to give you.

4

From Adoption Decision to Adoption Placement

Adoption is always an act of faith. It is a process that you cannot totally control. We have spent a good many pages describing the kinds of activities and information that help you know your family. We have given you an idea of the kind of children waiting for adoption. We have described various ways to adopt and presented general information about agencies. By this time you have probably gathered much additional information about your local situation and adoption. It is time now when you must make a two-part decision. Will you proceed to adopt a child? If so, who will you add to your family? This decision must be made with as much information and thought as possible but always with the knowledge that all things are not under our control.

Making the Adoption Decision

If you have decided to adopt through an agency, the process of making your decision will be assisted by your agency. If you are arranging an independent adoption, the process will be much the same, but the part of the agency must be played by you in addition to your role as the potential adopting family. This chapter will carry the adoption process from the decision to adopt some child to the placement of a particular child in your home for the purpose of adoption.

Making both parts of the adoption decision involves you and your spouse, the rest of your family, and the agency. Because you are a Christian, at every point you will be seeking the will and wisdom of God. The decision to adopt will involve going back over all that you have learned about yourself and adoption and applying hard thinking to your situation.

The Role of Your Family

It is likely that one person in your family has gathered most of the information about adoption, probably discussing what was found with a spouse. If you have not already done so, it is time to think about the role of your children and extended family members in making this decision. We asked adopting families, "What role did your extended family—siblings, parents, grandparents, and so on—have in the decision to adopt?" Some of their answers may be helpful to you. Most said that their extended family played no role at all in the decision. Some first announced the decision to their children or other relatives just before the adoptive child arrived in the family. Others waited until the child reached their home before telling family members of their plans. We have a sense that among these parents, they felt they had the right to make this decision alone and, having made it, that most of their families welcomed and supported the decision. But one added, "It wouldn't have made any difference if they had said no."

Thinking back on our own experience, our attitude the first time we adopted was much the same, although we did ask counsel from both sets of parents. Whether we actually factored their advice into our decision is less certain. In any case we went ahead over some cautionary advice, and our families, too, supported our decision.

From the standpoint of adults who are now grandparents, we have changed our views somewhat. It seems reasonable to give your extended family an opportunity to discuss this decision with you, for the child to be adopted becomes a part of that family. This is not to suggest that we must let others veto our decisions, but rather that open discussion of pros and cons, of feelings and hopes, of prejudices and misgivings, may prepare the way for later needs. A grandparent who is not consulted in advance may feel less able to accept the child wholeheartedly. The young parents may feel, "We asked for this; now we have to carry it alone," when they need help. Your own parents often know you better than you think and can provide valuable insights into your self-assessment or into the nature of the community into which you will take your adopted child. Discussion of adoption plans with them is usually a resource that should not be ignored as you consider adoption. When we adopted our second child, we had four older children to consult. This time it was truly a family decision, and we believe those discussions have been a strong factor in the successful development by our son of sibling relationships as well as the parent-child bonds.

How Can the Agency Help in the Decision?

Self-assessment. The most important contribution the agency can make is to provide you with the tools for self-assessment. Their personnel cannot decide whether you should adopt, because they cannot know even a small part of what is true about you. But they can help you find out what adoption requires and whether you have the talents, strength, and motivations to adopt. Some of the tools that are available have already been suggested in chapter 2. Your agency will have others. If you have chosen to work with an agency, its personnel will take you through a self-assessment process designed to help you decide whether you should adopt and what kind of children would best fit into your family.

Adoption group. The agency also can recommend adoption self-study groups. You may be helped best if you can be put in touch with other Christians who have some of the same motivations and reservations that you have, but you can learn a great deal about adoption and about yourself by working with all kinds of adoptive parents. Among those who have already experienced adoption, some will have had an easy time and some will be facing up to big and little disappointments. Others, like your-selves, may be brand-new to the idea. In the interchange of ideas and experience, especially with a skillful group leader present, you can learn a lot about what adoption is really like and what kind of characteristics you are going to need to make a reason-able success of this role of parent. Five or six sessions are probably adequate, though many couples find it helpful to con-tinue in a group of adoptive parents through the adoption pro-cess and on into the post-adoption years. Not all groups are equally successful, and some parents find that the required ses-sions are a chore. If your group experience is negative, be sure to take a hard look at what is bothering you about what you heard or felt there.

Agency screening. The agency also has a role in your decision in terms of "screening out and screening in." Most agencies agree that there is a child somewhere for any parents who sincerely want to adopt. But you may also decide at some point in the process that you are not called to parent, especially as more information has become available to you. As previously men-tioned, the concept of matching parents to children has been updated to something far beyond eye color and intelligence scores. The aim of most agencies today is to screen in (that is, make available as potential adoptive parents) as high a propor-tion of applicants as possible, for they have many kinds of children to place. It will probably be up to you to screen yourself out of the prospective parent pool if you do not feel you have the characteristics needed for the available children.

The agency also has a responsibility to be honest with you. The social worker should share the results of any interviewing or testing done with you, and also be honest about the kinds of children available and the requirements they make on your fam-ily. You also need to know how the agency is going to help you through the years.

Biblical Decision Making

Christians have been promised by God that if they will seek his guidance in making decisions, he will provide wisdom.

Bible study. In chapter 2, in connection with self-assessment, we reminded you to continually bring your exploration of adoption motivations and capacities under the scrutiny of the Word of God. Now it is time to go back over your Bible study and sermon notes or your spiritual journal for the period. Look for counsel that God has given you during this time, for applications of Scripture to your situation, and for any direction God may have indicated. It is not an accident if your pastor has preached a series on a particular subject or your Bible study led you along an unexpected channel. If you have been seeking his will, God has been bringing his Word to bear on your situation. Be sure to open your mind to that teaching. As you mentally summarize what you have learned about yourselves and adoption, and what you have been hearing from the Word of God, the Holy Spirit will help you make the necessary applications to your decision.

Prayer. Your prayer time should take on a sense of urgency as you make the adoption decision. If you have shared your exploration with other Christians, now is the time to ask those close to you to pray with you about the decision. Ask specifically for help from God as you tell him which areas puzzle or concern you. In the familiar Old Testament story, King Hezekiah of Judah took the Assyrian ruler's threatening letter and "spread it before the LORD" (2 Kings 19:14). Certainly God already knew everything in that letter, but Hezekiah committed it to God's disposal. Perhaps you will want to write out the pros and cons that are in your mind as you try to decide about adoption, then deliberately speak them out loud as you pray with your spouse.

The counsel of other Christians, especially those who are your spiritual leaders, also has a part to play in Christian decision making. Perhaps you have already talked with some as you gathered information. If you have thoroughly explored your situation, you and they may feel that they know less than you do about making this decision. So why bother? Whether or not they have specific advice or ideas to offer, there is blessing to be found in opening up our lives to other Christians and letting them be involved with us. You will feel closer to your leaders and more able to share the joys and difficulties of rearing your adopted children if you include them now in your decision making.

Sanctified common sense. Christians' decision making also includes a large measure of what we refer to as "sanctified common sense." During the process of investigating adoption, you have probably had emotional ups and downs, have considered some actions that are rather off the wall, and have had times when you wondered if you should just give up the whole thing and concentrate on enjoying life without the hassle of children. Now it is time to forget all those extremes of emotional response and look sensibly and thoroughly at your situation and what you have to offer, at the children available, and at what you really want to do, now that you have the facts on hand. You have investigated, you have listened for God's direction, you have prayed—now use the mind God gave you to arrive at a conclusion. Having done so, you are ready to move forward toward adoption—or in a different direction entirely, at least until something quite definite changes in your lives.

What Child?

Assuming that you have decided *for* adoption, you are now ready to consider whether you should adopt a particular child or a particular sibling group. Having decided that you want to add to your family by adoption, the decision-making process has to be renegotiated with the characteristics of a particular child in mind. (We will not continue to say "children," although it is possible you have decided you could accept more than one child at a time.)

This decision will arise when the agency calls and says, "We have a child we want you to consider," or when you locate a possible adoptee if you are working independently. This is both an exciting and frightening piece of news. All the planning and working now come together at a particular point, and you are about to make a decision that will greatly affect your life and the life of an unknown child for many years to come. How much we need the assurances of the love and help of God at such a time! Let's go through the decision-making steps again, this time with a specific child in mind.

The Role of Your Family

If you are a couple without children, the decision to accept a particular child is probably made almost totally by the two of you. It seems unfair to a child to parade him before relatives and ask them to help you decide whether this child should join your family. If you have discussed the general characteristics of children you are going to consider (age range, race, possible mental or physical disabilities, sex), it seems unnecessary to involve a lot of people in choosing to accept a particular child. Naturally, if talking things over with someone helps you clarify your own thinking, that would be helpful. But, fundamentally, you are going to live with this child as his parents, and it is you who must decide if you will respond well to a particular personality and set of characteristics.

If there are other children in the family, they should be involved in the process of getting to know this child. Their first reactions may be either strongly positive or strongly negative, or they may even try to refuse to get involved in the choice at all. Children should not be given veto power over decisions that are properly those of adults, but as you see these reactions you can deal with them to some extent before the adopted child is in your home. All people, including children, cooperate better when they are given input into decision-making processes. You may save yourself and the newcomer many unpleasant scenes if you give attention to preparing your own children for the arrival of this new brother or sister. You will find additional help in chapter 6, "Welcoming a New Member." I (Evelyn) shall never forget the baffled look on the face of a ten-year-old only child. I was there when she was informed for the first time that from that moment on she would be sharing her room with the two-year-old adopted sister she had just met.

Some personal histories of adopting families include cases where the extended family has not accepted either the decision to adopt or adoption of a particular child. You must consider what you will do if that should happen in your case. For example, what will you do if you have decided to adopt a biracial child, your family has said little in advance, and now the grandparents or an aunt and uncle and their children ignore or are unfair to this child? Some parents have told us it was not a serious problem as long as they had little contact with those family members. Sometimes miles helped minimize the problem. Occasionally the families just made a stated or implied decision not to spend time together. No one can tell you what you should do in this case. Remember that you may be able to ignore the opinions and actions of others from a position of adult security, but the child you are adopting may be very sensitive and hurt by exclusion. That such situations should arise in Christian families is evidence of sin, but you cannot ignore the possibility. You must be prepared to deal wisely with the facts of the problem. It is unfair to make a child the brunt of a battle fought on adult ground.

The Role of the Agency

The most important responsibility of the agency when its personnel begin to discuss a particular child for your family is to be totally honest with you about the child.

Accurate information. From time to time we read in the local newspaper descriptions of children available for adoption. Some would be humorous if the underlying reality were not so tragic. A child who has been bounced around for years is described as "friendly and outgoing." Behind such a description lies the fact that this child, after years of rejection, may very well be incapable of close relationships. To manage in a nonaccepting environment, he has developed a friendly smile and manner that is projected toward one and all—but it may take years for an adoptive family to penetrate that protective surface and find the lonely child who needs to love and trust a special someone. Another child is described as "somewhat behind in school, since she has been frequently moved in the past but has tested in the normal intelligence range." The toughest children to teach in many a classroom have normal intelligence. Chances are, this child has either missed basic instruction in some areas or has emotional problems that make it impossible for her to concentrate on schoolwork. Realistically, she is going to need a lot of help and may never reach the potential that those tests seem to indicate. Are we suggesting that you not adopt such children? Not at all. But the agency has a fair amount of information about the likely consequences of past experiences in the life of the child. It has a duty to be honest with you about the experiences and the kind of remedial effort needed and time likely to pass before those experiences fade. On that basis they can ask you to make a commitment to whatever it takes, and neither you nor the child needs to feel cheated in later years.

Specifically, it is our position that you should know everything the agency knows about the child's history and that it should make strenuous efforts to fill in all possible gaps before the adoption takes place. On the other hand, some unsupported rumor, wild allegations, or gratuitous remarks may have found their way into the social-work records. The agency is under no obligation to pass those along to you, and it would be well if such material could be permanently deleted from the child's file.

In gathering relevant information about the child, the agency should seek ethnic background, health records for one or more generations, records of other family members (such as brothers and sisters), school records, an accurate record of homes the child has lived in, names of significant people in the child's past, brushes with the law, and any other concrete information that might be helpful to the adopting parents or valuable to the child at a later date. One adoptive parent wrote: "Our child is an American Indian, at least in part. If his parentage were registered, he would be eligible for education benefits, but we don't have the records to establish his identity." Such records should be gathered and verified during the adoption process.

An adoption plan. The agency is responsible for arriving at a plan that enables you to get acquainted with the child and the child with you and his possible new home. This is a well-developed area in social-work practice. There are guidelines for what helps and hurts, and the agency should provide these guidelines and help carry out a good visitation plan before you make the decision. Details cannot be spelled out here, because every situation is different. Reading will help you decide what you want from the agency, in case those you are working with do not take a strong initiative in this area. Sometimes, in the press of time or financial crunch, agencies do not practice what they know is good policy, but if you know what you need and ask for it, they will provide it if possible. What happened *before* the child comes to live in your home has tremendous effect on what follows, especially if you are adopting an older child.

The match. Although you will participate in the decision about whether to take a particular child, it is the ultimate responsibility of the agency to decide whether or not a particular child should be placed in your home for adoption. Even if you adopt independently, at some point a court will probably appoint a social worker to review your situation. Probably you will reach an amicable agreement. Obviously if you say "No," they will not be able to force a child on you. On the other hand, if they say "No," it is unlikely that you will get the child. Naturally there are exceptions in which court cases have been fought. Sometimes adoptive parents win; more often the agencies do. We think you should try to avoid such situations because the child gets hung up in limbo while the courts make their ponderous way through the mess.

Support services. It is the responsibility of the agency to arrange for any support services that may be needed to assure the success of the adoption or the remediation of problems the child may already have. These include medical subsidies, counseling arrangements, working with schools to arrange tutoring services, special community services for mentally or physically disabled children, and so on. The adopting family will gradually assume primary responsibility for these functions, but since the agency knows the community-service ropes, and you probably do not, it helps to have agency social workers assist you as you make these connections. If you need but are not getting that kind of help, be sure to ask for it. In some agencies the crying baby gets the bottle. With limited resources, it is bound to be that way.

Can you say no? The agency and its workers have the responsibility to respect the previous guidelines you have set up together about the characteristics of a child you will accept. Occasionally a family is asked to adopt a child who is totally outside their planning and expectations. Sometimes the agency is desperate for a family, has no "suitable" child waiting for a home like yours, and decides to explore your family for a child they do have. Such an overture should be just that—an exploratory question. You may decide to expand the categories you can accept, but you should be quite hesitant to do this purely on the basis of picturing in your mind a particular waiting child. Your emotions may get in the way of a good decision. If you are feeling some pressure from the agency, this is a good response: "We really did consider a child that old [or whatever the characteristic is] and decided it wouldn't work for us. We are willing to give it some more thought, but we would like to do it without knowing any more about a specific child. If we conclude we could take an older child after all, we will let you know and perhaps you will have one suitable for us then." This does not close the door to the possibility that God may be asking you to reconsider your guidelines, and it lets the agency know you are willing to work further with them. But it puts no one in a pressure bind for a quick decision.

The agency should never make you feel that it is "this child or none" and usually will not intentionally do so. If for some reason that is the way it sounds to you, be honest with the agency. Don't, for example, take an older child in the hopes that the agency will then appreciate your help and give you a baby! That sounds quite ridiculous, but there is a perception that such things do happen. The agency may press quite hard for you to accept an older child and discourage you from hoping for an infant. If you continue to believe that it is important to you and God's will for you to have an infant, be patient. God will time things perfectly.

God and Your Decision

As in the first decision point, when you had to choose whether to go ahead with adoption, you have now come to a point when

you must seek spiritual direction. You must decide whether God
is asking you to accept a particular boy or girl as your child. For
some, that decision will seem crystal-clear, and you will have only
to thank God for making his will known to you. Others may be
overwhelmed with feelings of doubt and even wonder if they
should adopt at all. It is time to rethink what you have learned
about adoption and about yourself in the light of the Word of
God. It is time to pray, talking to the Lord about this specific child,
about your doubts, the things that encourage you, and the fears
you have, as well as the possibilities.

If you have uncertainty, it may be time to seek again the
counsel of others. As you put into words all the things you are
thinking, you may see more clearly. No one else can make this
decision, but a godly counselor who knows you well can help
you sort through your situation. We believe that if you sincerely
seek to know and do God's will, he will make it sufficiently plain
that you will be able to act. That does not mean you will never
again have doubts about this action. But you will be able to look
back and say, "I know that at the time we made this choice, we
looked to God for help and we did obey the direction he gave."
That confidence will help in periods of discouragement and
doubt. You will be able to say with Hannah: "I prayed for this
child, and the LORD has granted me what I asked of him" (1 Sam.
1:27, NIV).

5

Legal Aspects of Adoption
Ruth Felker Kolb

Adoption is the legal creation of a new family. While in some cases the adoption is a first step in the formation of the parent-child relationship, in others, the adoption is the legal recognition of a relationship that already exists. In every case, the creation of a new legal family requires the dissolution of another family and shifting of rights and responsibilities regarding the child.

Adoption has several legal consequences. The adopted child has the right to the adopted family's name, the right of care and support from the adopted family, the right to inherit from the adopted family, and the right to recover damages in a suit for the wrongful death of his adoptive parents. The adopted child in turn has legal responsibility for supporting his adoptive parents if they are unable to care for themselves in older age. Conversely, the

This chapter was written by Ruth Felker Kolb, Juris Doctorate, with editorial contributions by D. W. and E. H. Felker. Ms. Kolb is a member of the Pennsylvania Bar and has a special interest in family law.

child's birth family is no longer responsible for the care of the child and has no right of support from the child. However, in some states the child retains the right to inherit through his birth family. The legal institution of adoption in primitive form can be traced to pre-Roman times, but the first thorough development of adoption law was Roman. Roman law recognized two forms of adoption: *adoptio* and *androgatio*. *Adoptio*, the precursor of modern adoption, involved the transfer of rights and responsibilities of an un-emancipated child's birth father to the adoptive father. *Androgatio* was the adoption of an adult and was done primarily for inheritance purposes. Adult adoption still exists and is less complex than the adoption of a minor.

Today, United States adoption procedure is found in state law. Although attempts have been made to nationalize the adoption process through the passage of uniform adoption laws, adoption still varies from state to state. Likewise, the procedure in international adoption varies from country to country.

In order to complete a valid adoption, the procedure outlined in the pertinent adoption legislation must be meticulously followed. Any departure from the prescribed procedure can be grounds for a court's refusal to grant a final adoption decree or, in extreme cases, for invalidating a final decree.

Despite the variation in law from state to state, adoption does follow a general pattern. This chapter gives a brief outline of this pattern. A more detailed explanation of the issues of consent, termination of parental rights, agency investigations, and placement with the adoptive parents is given in subsequent sections. However, one of the first tasks for adoptive parents is choosing and working with an attorney.

Choosing an Attorney

Choosing a qualified and competent attorney is a vital part of the adoption process. The best source of information regarding attorneys in your area is your own family attorney. If an adoption is uncontested by the birth parents, it is a routine legal process that any attorney can handle. If the adoption might be contested, however, you should ask your attorney if she or he is comfortable handling the case and discuss the advisability of hiring an attorney who specializes in family law. As a general rule, even a contested adoption does not involve complicated legal issues that are beyond the scope of expertise of most attorneys. If your family does not have general legal counsel, this is a good time to establish a relationship with an attorney. Ask for recommendations from friends, family, or from attorneys you know socially. Another source of information is the local bar association.

To begin the process, telephone the attorneys you are considering and explain that you are contemplating adoption and are looking for an attorney to handle the adoption as well as other legal needs that may arise, such as drafting a will and handling your estate. If you are the type of client that the attorney handles, ask if you could meet to discuss fees and determine whether to establish an attorney-client relationship.

At the meeting ask what type of work the firm is involved in and discuss the type of legal advice you expect to need. As you talk, try to assess whether you feel comfortable with and could work together with this person over a long period of time in a variety of situations. If your impression is favorable, discuss fees for the adoption and other work. The reputation of the attorney and your impressions are more valuable pieces of information than the cost of services. Thorough, precise, skilled legal advice from someone you respect and trust is worth infinitely more than a cut-rate, slipshod piece of legal work from someone who is difficult to work with. If the fees seem substantially higher or lower than what friends and family have paid, ask the attorney why this is so.

At the end of the meeting, tell the attorney that you and your spouse would like to discuss the matter alone and that you will let the attorney know your decision. Once you have determined the attorney who will handle your adoption, meet again and ask for an explanation of the adoption process. Additionally, you may wish to request a copy of the statutes covering adoption in your state and county. Request a photocopy of any correspondence or papers that are filed with the court on your behalf. Remember, this is *your* adoption and you are paying for these services. Since a good attorney will be happy to provide information and to answer all of your questions throughout the adoption process, –ASK! In this chapter, I will be mentioning specific issues to raise and questions to ask, but be sure to ask any other questions that occur to you.

A *note of caution*: In the unlikely event that an attorney advises you to withhold information, alter facts, or tell a lie, do not do it. This type of conduct could make the adoption invalid. Because no reputable attorney engages in dishonest practices, terminate the relationship and report the attorney to the local bar association.

In addition to attorneys representing the adoptive parents, and in some cases the birth parents and the agency, some states provide for the independent appointment by the court of a *guardian ad litem* to represent the child, especially in cases where the adoption is contested. Often the *guardian ad litem* will conduct an independent investigation and assessment and make a recommendation to the court regarding the child's best interests. This recommendation is another factor for consideration by the judge.

Adoption Proceedings

Petition

Adoption proceedings are initiated when the adoptive parents file a petition for adoption. Most statutes outline the information that must be in the petition and require that the petition be signed and verified by the adoptive parents. The statute should be strictly and exactly followed. In some states the child must live with the adoptive parents for a stated period of time prior to filing the petition. In other states the petition may be filed but a hearing or the entering of a final decree of adoption follows a prescribed time period.

Hearing

If the adoption is uncontested, the adoption hearing is a routine proceeding in which the judge determines whether the statute has been complied with in regard to the consent of the birth parents or the termination of parental rights, and the filing of the adoption petition. The judge then considers the recommendation, if any, of a social-services agency or *guardian ad litem* and determines if the adoption is in the child's best interests. The adoptive parents are often required to be present, presumably so the judge can be satisfied that they will be suitable parents. Under some statutes, the child must be present, at least when old enough so that his consent to the adoption is required. The adoption hearing is often private and may occur in the judge's chambers. The hearing is informal, and rules of evidence are not strictly observed. For example, when my younger brother was adopted, the hearing was held in the judge's chambers. All paperwork had been submitted in advance, and no clerks, lawyers, or social workers were present. All our family were seated conversationally in his office, and we spent fifteen or twenty minutes getting acquainted and discussing our family plans informally. Four-year-old Jeff spent most of the hearing securely perched in the judge's lap. After a friendly visit, the judge called in the appropriate clerk and gave her directions in the form of legal orders. He told Jeff he was now officially Jeffrey William Felker, shook hands all around and our family went out to celebrate.

The petitioner, i.e., the adoptive parents, has the burden of proof—normally not a critical factor except when the adoption is contested. If the adoption *is* contested, the procedure will be much more formal; a court record will be made and the rules of evidence more strictly followed.

Agency Reports

In many states the court is required to consider the recommendations of an agency investigation in determining whether to grant the petition. If the agency report recommends the adoption, no problems arise for the adoptive parent in this respect.

If the agency recommends against adoption, the adoptive parents must be provided with a copy of the report and have an opportunity to rebut its contents. This opportunity may include the right to cross-examine the social worker who compiled the report and may extend to the right to examine persons giving information to the social worker. In some states the report is rebutted by presenting evidence of the fitness of the adoptive parents. Although a negative recommendation is cause for concern, the judge, not the agency makes the final determination, and the adoptive parents may be able to show why the recommendation should be disregarded. A relatively simple example is a case where the agency recommends against adoption due to the age of the adoptive parents. Although it may be against agency policy to recommend adoptions by older parents, a judge may determine that this adoption is in the child's best interests. Although agencies may have standards or rules regarding age, marital status, financial status, or religious affiliation, these rules are generally not part of adoption statutes and therefore are not binding on the judge.

Interlocutory and Final Decree

In order to provide the court and/or the agency an opportunity to evaluate the adoption before it becomes final, many states permit a court to enter an interlocutory decree of adoption, with the final decree to be entered at a later time, usually six months. The interlocutory decree gives the adoptive parents custody of the child and imposes upon them the obligations of parents. Because it is not final, it may be revoked by the court if there is good cause.

The final decree of adoption is permanent and ends the child's legal rights and duties with respect to his birth parents and creates new rights and duties with respect to the adoptive parents. The final decree may also contain a provision changing the child's name and authorizing that a new birth certificate be issued and that all the records regarding the adoption be sealed.

If the court does not enter a final adoption decree, a decision must be made regarding custody of the child. The judge may make the decision then or may order a new hearing to decide the custody issue.

Consent

Adoption statutes require the consent of birth parent(s), guardian(s), or other person in the position of parent as a prerequisite to adoption—unless statutory exceptions exist, such as abandonment, neglect, mental illness, or other grounds for terminating parental rights or waiving the consent requirement.

The consent must be in writing and often must be witnessed and notarized or acknowledged. Some statutes also prescribe the timing for obtaining the consent. For example, consent in some states may not be obtained before the child is born or must be obtained at least seventy-two hours after the birth of the child. The formalities surrounding consent are designed to protect the rights of the birth parent and to obtain a consent that is well considered and unlikely to be revoked. These formalities must be followed to the letter, and there are numerous cases where the adoption petition was not granted because of a failure to follow the procedures outlined in the statute.

When my brother Donald was adopted, our family hit a legal snag at what was supposed to be the final hearing. The court determined that a statutory requirement to advertise a notice to a birth parent (whose address was unknown) had not been met. The hearing was adjourned, and the agency and lawyers were ordered to fulfill this requirement before requesting a new hearing. Several months later the adoption hearing was held and the decree granted, but the original failure to fulfill the statute could not be overlooked by the court.

There are also cases where courts have not required strict compliance in order to effectuate the intent of the parties and the purposes of the adoption statute. However, these exceptions are few in number, and a failure to follow procedures is a risky gamble at best.

Persons seeking to adopt should ask their lawyer what the requirements for consent are in their state. Adoptive parents should ask whether each step has been followed and request a copy of the consent. The solution to every possible problem involving consent is beyond the scope of this chapter, and the best protection for the adoptive parents and the child is the counsel of their attorney.

Unmarried fathers. A particularly troublesome area of adoption is the consent of the unmarried father. Until 1972 the typical adoption statute allowed an adoption to proceed without the consent of a father who was not married to the mother of the child. It was assumed that if the father was not married to the mother, he was irresponsible and unconcerned about his child. The unmarried father was disregarded by the law, and the child was considered the child of only the mother.

In 1972 the Supreme Court of the United States departed from tradition and previous court decisions and, in the case of *Stanley* v. *Illinois*, ruled that the father of an illegitimate child has some rights to the child under the due-process and equal-protection clauses of the Constitution. The *Stanley* case raised the issue of a father's rights in the context of a custody proceeding following the death of the children's mother. Although Stanley had lived with the children and provided support, the Illinois custody statute at issue in the case did not include the unwed father under its definition of "parent." The Supreme Court held the statute unconstitutional as applied to Stanley.

The question of the rights of an unwed father in the context of an adoption proceeding was not considered by the Supreme Court until 1978, when it heard the case of *Quillion* v. *Walcott*. This case was a constitutional challenge to a Georgia statute that did not recognize the parental rights of an unwed father unless he took steps to legitimate the child. The law allowed an illegitimate child to be adopted with the consent of the mother alone, and only she had the exclusive power to veto the adoption. Nearly thirteen years after the birth of the child, the unwed father sought to legitimate the child and block the adoption of the child by the mother's husband of ten years. The unwed father argued that he should have the same power to veto the adoption as was provided to the mother and to married or divorced parents, unless he was found to be unfit as a parent. The Supreme Court disagreed and ruled that the court needed only to find that the adoption and denial of legitimacy were in the child's best interests. The Supreme Court distinguished the two cases on the basis of the role of the father in the child's life and limited the application of *Stanley* to cases in which the father had "been a *defacto* member of the child's family unit."

In 1979 the Supreme Court in *Cabon* v. *Mohammed* declared unconstitutional a New York statute that made a distinction between the rights of unmarried mothers and unmarried fathers. The Supreme Court declared it unconstitutional because the distinction was not related to the state's interest in adoption. The father had been a *defacto* member of the family unit, the parents had declared themselves married, the father was listed on the birth certificate and supported the children. However, the State of New York ruled that as an unwed father he had no authority to prevent an adoption. The Supreme Court noted that the statute would have allowed even an uncaring, alienated mother to arbitrarily exclude from participation in an adoption decision a loving father who exhibited a "significant parental interest in the child."

The deciding factor in each of the cases of *Stanley, Quillion,* and *Cabon* was the father's relationship to and degree of involvement with his children. Still left unclear was whether the unmarried father had an absolute right to notice and opportunity to be heard at the adoption hearing of his illegitimate child. Was it necessary for the trial court in every adoption involving an unmarried father to locate the father, establish whether the father was a *"defacto* member of the child's family unit" or had showed a "significant parental interest in the child"? If this was not required, what were the minimum constitutional protections guaranteed to the unmarried father?

In another case the Supreme Court addressed the question of whether the unmarried father had a constitutional right to notice and an opportunity to be heard at the adoption of his illegitimate child. The Court in *Lehr* v. *Robertson* (1983) again emphasized the relationship of rights and responsibilities with regard to the child. In *Lehr,* as in *Quillion,* the father had not demonstrated a commitment to the responsibilities of parenting. The Court ruled that where a father does not take advantage of opportunities to develop a parent-child relationship, such as providing financial and emotional support, participating in legitimization proceedings or entering his name in an available registry, the father does not have an automatic constitutional right to notice and an opportunity to be heard.

Although this decision expedited the adoption of illegitimate children in cases where the father had shown no interest in the child, many questions remain unanswered. What about situations in which the mother refuses to allow the unmarried father to establish a relationship with the child? What about the adoption of newborns? The decision to have an abortion does not require the father's consent. Should the decision to bear the child and place it immediately for adoption require his consent? What effect will the fact that the father provided financial support during pregnancy have on his rights?

Because these questions remain unanswered, some agencies are taking a conservative position and making considerable efforts to locate every father and obtain his consent. Consequently, the adoptions of many children have been delayed several months. This is especially regrettable in the case of newborn adoptions, where the best alternative is certainly a permanent, adoptive placement from birth.

Although the Supreme Court has not heard such a case, there is the potential for a case in which an adoption was overturned because of a challenge by an unmarried father. Accordingly, care should be taken to preserve the rights of unmarried fathers to the greatest extent possible in a particular situation. Certainly the written consent of the unmarried father should be obtained wherever possible. If it is not available, the adoptive parents should know why it is not available. Is the father unidentified, purposely unavailable, or denying paternity? Or is the father interested in the birth of the child, providing emotional and financial support to the mother, and opposed to the adoption? The reason that the consent is not available determines the degree of legal risk to the adoptive parents. Again, every situation is different, and adoptive parents need to be informed of their particular situation, but for certain—if the father's consent is not included—*ask some questions!*

Consent of the child. In some states the consent of a child above a certain age, often twelve or fourteen, is also necessary before an adoption can proceed. A court with no such statutory directive, or in the case of a younger child, may consider the wishes of the child but is not bound by them.

Revocation of consent. After a valid consent has been properly obtained from all of the necessary parties, another question arises. Under what circumstances can the birth parents change their mind and revoke their consent? A situation in which this happens is certainly a traumatic experience for adoptive parents and often poses great harm to the child as well. Courts and the adoption statutes that address the issue are primarily concerned with the best interests of the child and secondarily with the birth parents' rights. Little, if any, consideration is given to the adoptive parents because—until the adoption decree is final—the adoptive parents have virtually no legal rights regarding the child.

There are a variety of approaches to the issue of whether consent may be withdrawn. One approach is that consent may be revoked only with the approval of the court, which implies that the court may scrutinize the birth parent's reason for revoking. Another approach is that consent may be revoked only if it was given under duress or was fraudulently obtained. *Fraud* and *duress* are legal terms that require a showing of particular circumstances. The court's primary concern is whether the mother *intended* to consent unconditionally to the adoption.

Another approach is to allow consent to be revoked only upon a finding that it is in the child's best interests. Still others follow the approach that consent may be withdrawn for any reason whatsoever until the adoption decree is final.

The tendency in most states is to allow consent to be withdrawn only with court approval. The court then considers all of the circumstances, such as the birth parent's reason for revoking consent, the circumstances under which consent was given, the age of the birth parent, the age of the child, the time that has elapsed, and whether the child had already been placed in the adoptive home. The welfare of the child is the court's primary concern.

Termination of Parental Rights
If birth parents refuse to consent to the adoption, or if for some

other reason their consent is unavailable, the court must usually terminate their parental rights without their consent before the adoption can proceed. Some states allow adoption where the consent is withheld by fit parents but contrary to the child's best interests; however, in most states the conduct of the birth parent is the determining factor. This means that a showing that the adoptive parents will be better parents than the birth parents is not enough. The petitioning party, often a public social-service agency, has the burden of proving that the birth parents are unfit, i.e., totally inadequate as parents. Most statutes stipulate abandonment, neglect, abuse or conduct endangering the welfare of the child, or some variation of these as evidence of parental unfitness. The statutes vary in the conduct listed, as well as in how the conduct is specifically defined. For example, two states may both include "neglect" in their statute but define the term very differently.

Abandonment is a common ground for termination and is defined as the complete denial of all parental responsibilities, with the intent of never resuming them. The intent of the parent to permanently sever ties is the determining factor. Consequently, the voluntary placement of a child in foster care or with relatives even for a number of years is not "abandonment." Even minimal inquiries or contact evidencing some parental concern (such as a phone call to a social worker or a postcard to the child) will prevent a finding of abandonment. In some cases, when a birth parent revokes consent to the adoption, the adoption proceeds on the grounds that the original consent was an abandonment of the child. The outcome hinges on whether it was the intent of the birth parent to unconditionally place the child for adoption at the time the consent was given.

Neglect, another common ground for termination of parental rights, is less susceptible to definition than abandonment. Certainly the failure to provide for a child's most basic physical needs constitutes neglect, but what of emotional neglect or care that is adequate for most children but is neglectful of this child's particular needs? Similarly, abuse, although easily defined in extreme cases, may also be difficult to define in other instances. Both neglect and abuse may be difficult to prove in a court of law following strict standards of evidence.

Mental illness may be included in the statute as grounds for termination of parental rights if the parent is permanently unable to care for the child.

In conclusion, the termination of parental rights will vary from state to state in terms of the conduct of the parents necessary to terminate rights, the persons who may bring an action to terminate parental rights, and the form of the hearing. If the termination of their rights is vigorously opposed by the parents, this can be a lengthy and often unsuccessful process. Courts are extremely reluctant to sever the birth-parental relationship. Even in cases where the child has been in foster care or in other care away from the birth parents, and it is clear that the child will probably never return to the birth parents, the court will often refuse to terminate parental rights.

Before planning to adopt a child whose birth parents are unwilling to consent to the adoption, the adoptive parents should be aware of the evidence to be used in the termination proceeding and meet with their attorney to assess the strengths and weaknesses of the case and the likelihood of success. Before deciding to pursue termination of parental rights, the parties may also want to consider the availability of other options such as guardianship, open adoption, or long-term foster care. Whenever possible, these decisions should be made prior to the placement of the child in your home so that everyone, including the child, has clear expectations. In any case, the termination of parental rights is rarely a "sure thing" in legal terms and represents an emotionally difficult process for the adoptive family and for the child.

Placement Process

Once the child is free for adoption, either by the consent of the birth parents or the termination of their parental rights, the courts must next determine the suitability of the adoptive family before issuing the adoption decree. The two steps—dissolving the birth family and creating a new family—may occur at one hearing or involve two separate hearings. The adoption placement may be made before any hearing, between two hearings, or after the adoption decree is issued, depending on agency policy and state law.

As mentioned previously, in determining the suitability of the adoptive family, a court will often be directed by the statute to consider the recommendation of a social-services agency. The court may also question the adoptive parents or other persons and, if necessary, the adoptive parents may present evidence in support of their petition.

In practical terms, the decision to place a particular child in a particular family is not made by the court but by the birth parents, the adoptive parents, and possibly an agency. The court then approves or disapproves of the placement decision

The methods of matching children with adoptive parents are varied. The three general categories are agency adoptions, independent adoptions, and black-market adoptions. An *agency adoption* is one in which a licensed public or private social-services agency places the child in an adoptive home. An *independent adoption* is one in which the child is placed by the birth parents or some private individual, often a doctor or an attorney. A *black-market adoption* is an independent adoption where someone, either the birth parents or a middle man, or both, profits from the adoptive parents' payment for the child.

Some states permit only agency adoptions, while other states require an agency review of the adoptive home in independent placements. Still others allow independent placements with review by the court. There has been a trend toward eliminating independent adoptions in order to solve the problem of black-market operations. The most common form of control of black-market adoptions is to require all parties to disclose to the court all monies paid and received. An adoptive parent should never fail to disclose all or part of a payment. An instruction to do so is an unethical act and should be reported to the court, a social-services agency, or an appropriate professional association.

Although state statutes are increasingly prescribing who may place children for adoption, there are few restrictions on whom children may be placed with, other than that they must be adults and, if married, both husband and wife must adopt the child. Rules or standards regarding age, marital status, and financial standing have their origin in agency policies, not in law.

The factors of race and religion have posed the most difficult placement problems. At one time, some states prohibited inter-racial adoptions altogether. Today, race or ethnic background is generally a factor to be considered along with all the other circumstances to determine whether the adoption is in the child's best interests. Another subject of controversy has been statutes that require children to be placed with persons or agencies of the same religion as the birth parents. As these statutes have been eroded on constitutional and policy ground, birth parents having a strong religious preference have relied on independent adop-tions and religiously affiliated agencies as a means of assuring the religious upbringing of their children.

A separate problem arises if adoptive parents feel they are the victims of religious discrimination in an agency's refusal to place a child in their home. Given the number of factors that must be considered in placing a particular child, it would be difficult to prove that religion alone was the factor in placing a child with another suitable family and that the agency erred in its considera-tion of the religion of the adoptive parents. Further, agencies are given broad discretion in the fulfillment of their duties. If adoptive parents believe that there is discrimination that is unrelated to the agency's interests in finding the best placement for a child, adoptive parents should consult with their attorney.

To summarize the adoption proceedings:

A hearing is held in which it is determined whether to sever the birth family and create a new family and enter an adop-tion decree.

The decree may be interlocutory and become final at a later time.

If the birth parents do not consent to the adoption their rights must be terminated. This may occur at the adoption hearing or may occur at a separate hearing.

The placement of a child in a prospective adoptive home may occur at various points in the adoption process.

Children may be placed by agencies, birth parents, or other private individuals.

International Adoption

The procedures for an international adoption are more complex than those previously outlined, because the adoption involves United States immigration law, the law of the country where the child was born, and the law of the state in which the adoptive parents live.

United States immigration law, which is found in the Immigration and Naturalization Act (hereinafter "Act") determines whether a child may enter the United States. As part of its provisions, the Act requires that all applicable state and foreign adoption laws be strictly followed. Although the Act itself is consistent for all individuals, state and foreign adoption laws vary.

United States Immigration and Naturalization Act

Under the Act, the adopting parents initiate the adoption and immigration process for the child by filing a "Petition to Classify an Orphan as an Immediate Relative." Known as an I-600 petition, this allows the child to enter the United States without regard to the normal numerical limitations imposed on immigrants.

The I-600 petition must include substantial information concerning the adoptive parents, including proof of United States citizenship and marital status, fingerprinting, and a favorable home study by a licensed agency. The home study must contain an evaluation of the adopting parents' capabilities to rear and educate the child, a description of their current residence and of the proposed residence of the child, and a statement signed by the appropriate agency official recommending the adoption. If the adoption will occur in the United States, an agency within the adoptive parents' state must do the study, but if the adoption occurs abroad, any agency licensed in the United States may do the study.

The I-600 petition must also contain information about the child. The primary requirement is that the child must be an "orphan" within the meaning of the Act. The Act defines an orphan as a child under sixteen years of age (when the petition is filed) who "is an orphan because of the death or disappearance of, abandonment or desertion by, or separation or loss from, both parents, or for whom the sole or surviving parent is incapable of providing the proper care and has in writing irrevocably released the child for emigration and adoption." Although fairly clear, some ambiguity exists about when a child has been unconditionally abandoned within the meaning of the Act. Therefore, the family history of the child's family must be researched to assure that the child meets the definition of "orphan."

The I-600 petition must also include the child's birth certificate, evidence of orphan status, and—if the adoption occurs abroad—a certified copy and translation of the adoption degree. The adoption decree will not be viewed as valid unless foreign law is complied with; as an additional requirement, the adoptive parents must personally observe the child prior to or during the adoption proceedings.

The Act allows advance processing of an incomplete I-600 petition where the child has not been identified and/or the home study completed. All other available information must be included, as well as such information as whether the child will be adopted in the United States or abroad, names of persons or agencies helping to locate a child, and where and when they intend to locate a child. The I-600 petition must be completed within one year or it will be considered abandoned.

After gathering the relevant information, the petitioners must submit original documents, verified by oath, with the petition to an Immigration and Naturalization Office. If the I-600 petition is approved, the child is given a medical examination and receives a visa from the United States consulate in his country. When the child arrives in the United States, the visa is replaced with an alien identification card proving legal residency. Until the child is naturalized, a separate bureaucratic process, he or she is an alien and does not enjoy all the rights and privileges of United States citizenship.

To initiate the naturalization process, the adoptive parents file Form N-402, "Application to Petition for Naturalization in Behalf of Child." The N-402 requires that the child be a lawful permanent resident and that he or she be adopted before becoming sixteen years old. It is not necessary for the child to take the oath of allegiance or to have a knowledge of English, as is required of adults seeking citizenship. The adoptive parents next file Form N-407, "Petition for Naturalization," in the Naturalization Court. This court then issues a certificate of naturalization. If an international adoption is done through an agency, the agency will assist the adopting parents in completing the necessary paperwork. In the case of an independent international adoption, the adopting parents' attorney can guide them through this complex (and at times overwhelming) process.

Foreign Law

Whether a child is free to be adopted and to emigrate from his country of origin is determined by the law of that country. There are generally two methods of international adoption followed by foreign countries, although other methods exist. In one method, exemplified by the laws of South Korea, an agency authorized by the country in which the child resides certifies that the adopting parents are suitable and able to provide for the child's needs. After consent is obtained from the birth parents or other suitable persons, the agency assumes guardianship of the child and transfers the child to the adoptive parents, who then complete the adoption in their home state.

Under the second method, often employed by South American countries, the parents travel to the country in which the child resides and personally file the adoption petition, along with verifying documents such as a birth certificate. A home study may also be required. Some countries retain continuing control for a specified time period after the adoption.

State Law

If the adoption is completed in the United States, the procedure will be the same as for other adoptions in the state. State law will also determine whether a foreign adoption is valid. As a general rule, an adoption that is valid in the country where it is done (already a requirement of immigration law) will be recognized by a state. Adoptive parents may wish to "refinalize" or simply readopt the child in their home state to assure the validity of the adoption.

While the federal government grants the right of United States citizenship with all of its benefits, state law grants additional rights, including the right to the adoptive parents' name, the right to support and to inherit from the adoptive parents, and the right to recover damages in a suit for the parents' wrongful death.

Open Adoption

Sometimes the term "open adoption" refers to a situation in which the birth parents know who has adopted their child but do not necessarily have contact with the child. However, in the following discussion, open adoption will be defined as an adoption in which it is agreed that the adopted child will have continuing contact with members of the birth family after the adoption is completed.

Open adoption is a relatively recent development in adoption law, and many states do not provide for open adoption in their statutes. In the United States, adoption has generally required the severing of all ties with the biological family before establishing a new family. Although this model of adoption is not universal to all countries and cultures, it is firmly entrenched in our legal system. This may be due in part to the fact that adoption law has been influenced by property-law concepts, with the child treated as a form of chattel. In property law "single ownership" must be clearly established.

The agreement in open adoption is a written one and may provide for contact such as visitation, the exchange of information, and pictures or phone calls. The contact may be between the child and the birth parents, siblings, grandparents, more distant relatives, and even friends. The adoptive parents, the child (if old enough) or in some cases the child's *guardian ad litem*, and the birth parents would all sign the agreement after making a decision on the time, place, and type of contract. The agreement would be presented to the court during the adoption hearing and become part of the final decree of adoption. The court would retain jurisdiction, similar to a child-custody arrangement, and could modify the agreement if necessary.

Despite the unresolved legal status of open adoptions and the practical and legal difficulties that can arise (this will be discussed later in the chapter), open adoption may be the best alternative in some situations. The first is those situations in which a child may not be available for adoption unless the birth parents consent to the adoption, and an open adoption agreement may be the only terms under which they will give their consent. One example of this is when a birth parent has placed a child in foster care and is unable to care for the child but is unwilling to relinquish all parental rights. The birth parents may consent to the adoption if they can continue to visit the child as they have during the foster-care placement. Another example is after a divorce and re-marriage, when a stepparent wishes to adopt the child of a spouse, but the noncustodial birth parent is reluctant to sever all ties with the child.

In these examples a court could order the adoption without the parent's consent only after terminating parental rights. Without proof of such conduct as abandonment or neglect, the court will not terminate parental rights. Therefore, open adoption with the consent of the birth parent is the only viable legal option if the child is to be adopted.

The second situation in which open adoption may be necessary is when a court determines that the adoption is not in the child's best interests unless continued contact with members of the birth family is assured. For example, a court may find that it is essential that an older child who has been in foster care continue to visit siblings placed in other foster or adoptive families.

In conclusion, in any situation in which a child's best interests are served by an adoption with continuing contact with the birth family, an open adoption should be considered.

The American model of adoption, with its concurrent severing and creating of family ties, does have distinct advantages. The adoptive parents, who now have the responsibility of caring for a child, also have the unrestricted decision-making powers enjoyed by other parents. The integrity of the adoptive family is protected and decision making is simplified. The disadvantage is that the model is not broad enough to encompass the situations of many children, especially older children.

Given the lack of explicit direction in the statutes, courts must determine how to handle open adoptions. Some courts refuse to enter the adoption decree or to terminate parental rights, stating that the law does not allow the adoption or termination to be conditioned on other agreements requiring contact with the birth family. Other courts permit the adoption, but there is an understanding among the parties that the agreement is unenforceable. This means that if there were a problem, a court could not order the adoptive parents to honor the agreement. This is an area of law that is undergoing scrutiny by legislatures and the legal profession, so these issues may be resolved in the future.

If open adoption is planned, the following are some general guidelines and issues to consider:

The agreement should be written and signed by all parties. All of the parties should be involved in deciding the terms of the agreement and understand exactly what the agreement provides. The child should be included in discussions where practicable, and, if not already done, the parties should consider requesting the court to appoint a *guardian ad litem* to represent the child during negotiations. The adoptive parents and the birth parents should have separate legal counsel. Appropriate social-agency personnel should also be included in discussions.

Once an agreement is reached, it should be put in writing and should describe each of the parties and their relationships and outline in detail the type of contact. For example, a provision stating that the birth parents can visit the child is too vague and raises many questions. Can the birth parents visit the child where and whenever they wish? Can the adoptive parents refuse to bring the child for a visit? If so, under what circumstances? Can other parties be present at the visit, such as other relatives not parties to the agreement? Can the child refuse to attend visits? Who is responsible for transporting the child to and from visits?

The following issues should be discussed and resolved during negotiations:

1. What type of contact? Phone calls? Visits? Letters? Pictures?
2. How often will contact take place? Once a month, once a week, twice a year?
3. Who decides the specific time? Is it stated in the agreement, e.g., the third Tuesday of every month? Is it not stated but to be decided by the adoptive parents, the birth parents, the child, or by mutual agreement? If visits are missed, will they be made up? What is a valid reason for missing a visit? What about holidays and summer vacations—do they affect the visitation schedule?
4. Where will the visits take place? At the child's adoptive home? The adoption agency? The zoo? At the birth parent's home? May the birth parent take the child places?
5. What is the procedure if one party becomes dissatisfied with the arrangement? This is the most important aspect of the agreement, as it will determine how future conflict will be resolved.

An agreement may state that if a problem cannot be resolved, the parties may petition a court or request a specific third party to resolve the issue. However, the parties may wish to limit how the agreement may be modified and may try to anticipate certain situations. For example, the agreement may state that a party cannot petition for more contact than is provided in the agreement. Or the parties may wish to anticipate a move to another area by the birth parents or adoptive parents and state how a move would affect such terms of the agreement as frequency and place of visits or responsibility for transportation. If the birth parent has a history of drug or alcohol abuse, the parties may wish to include a provision stating that a visit may be terminated if it appears that the birth parent has been using drugs or alcohol or that a failure to "stay clean" nullifies the agreement. The agreement could anticipate the situation in which a child is upset by visits and could provide that a family counselor evaluate the child and decide if it is in the child's best interests for visits to continue.

It is impossible to anticipate every situation or to list every question that an adoptive parent should ask. It is discouraging to think about every "worst possible scenario" when everyone wants the situation to work out for the good of the child with no conflict or disagreement. However, there are few situations more disrupting to the child and to the adoptive family than a courtroom battle with the birth family, and every step should be taken to minimize this possibility.

Open adoptions are not suggested because they are easy for the adoptive parents but because they are often the only way to meet the needs of a specific child. Given the problems that can arise, adoptive parents may even decide that they cannot agree to the contact unless there is a provision that the adoptive parents may terminate the agreement for any reason, if in good faith they believe it is in the child's best interests. In any event, the agreement *must always* include a provision that any disagreement or modification of the agreement will not affect the validity and finality of the adoption or the custody of the child.

The Search for Birth Parents

Another area of adoption law undergoing change is the controversy over adopted children's access to information about their birth family. Like open adoption, the controversy centers on the extent to which adoption severs the child's ties to the birth family. Under the traditional model, at the time of adoption a new birth certificate containing the adoptive family's name is issued, and the child's original birth certificate, the court record of adoption proceedings, the adoption order, and (in some cases) the agency files are sealed. Access to these sealed records can only be obtained with a court order upon a showing of good cause. Good cause is very narrowly interpreted, although courts tend to relax restrictions if only nonidentifying information is requested or if the permission of the birth parents is obtained through an intermediary.

The Supreme Court of the United States has ruled that the adopted person has no constitutional right to information regarding the birth family. Consequently, adult adoptees have pushed for legislative reform. Legislatures are faced with trying to balance the adoptees' desire for information, the birth parents' right to privacy, and the adoptive families' need for family consistency and stability during the child's formative years. The state also has an interest in assuring that there is a full and honest disclosure of all pertinent information during the placement and adoption process. Most state legislatures have favored sealed records, although some have provided for the release of nonidentifying information. In conclusion, court records should not be relied upon as a source of information, especially identifying information.

Agencies are usually a better source of information, although agencies may also refuse to disclose identifying information. Whether an agency discloses such information depends upon state law, agency policy, the birth parents' wishes and the agency's assessment of a particular situation.

In addition to greater accessibility than court records, agency information is often more extensive and complete. Another advantage is that the agency can make discretionary decisions regarding the release of particular information to a particular adoptee, taking into account the circumstances. The agency can also provide counseling to the adoptee or the adoptive parents to help them handle the information. However, since many agencies continue to operate under the traditional model of severing all ties and maintaining complete secrecy, they are therefore a poor source of information—especially if the adoptee's real desire is not just for information but to meet one or both birth parents. Adoption registries may provide a solution. The registries facilitate meetings of adult adoptees and birth parents if both sides consent.

Adoptive parents should work to resolve some of these issues during the adoption process. The first step is to be familiar with state law and agency policy. The adoptive parents should then persistently request all available information regarding the birth family—especially medical histories. This way, close and caring individuals—the child's adoptive parents—can disclose information when they feel their child is ready and can help their child to deal with the information. The adoptive parents can also find out at the time of the adoption if the birth parents wish to have contact with the child when he becomes an adult. Plans can be made to file with a state or national registry. If adopting through an agency or private person, plans can also be made to have the person or agency act as an intermediary between the adoptee and the birth family.

Adoption Disruption

Whether a child can be removed from the adoptive family depends in part on how far the adoption has progressed. Until a final decree is issued, often several months after a child is placed in the adoptive home, plans for adoption can be stopped and the child removed from the adoptive home upon the request of the adoptive parents.

After the issuance of a final adoption decree, the adoptive parents must petition for an annulment of the adoption. An annulment is rarely allowed and usually involves failing to inform the adoptive parents of a severe medical condition or mental retardation. The adoption creates a parent-child relationship, and the adoptive parents always have the same options as birth parents, i.e., releasing for adoption or placing in foster care.

When deciding whether to adopt a child, the adoptive parents should not consent to the entry of a final adoption decree if they are uncertain about the adoption.

The issue of whether the birth parent can change his or her mind was previously discussed under "Consent." To review, until the entry of the final decree, a court will consider the birth parent's attempts to disrupt the adoption within the context of the child's best interests in light of all the circumstances. A few states allow the birth parent to withdraw consent without cause at any time before the final decree is issued.

Once the adoption is finalized, the adoption can be attacked only on very narrow limited ground, such as that consent was never obtained or was obtained through fraud or duress. Under these circumstances, the court may still uphold the adoption if it seems in the child's best interests. However, some courts will not uphold a birth parent's challenge to the adoption if the procedures outlined in the adoption statute were not followed.

Summary

Adoption law exists to protect the rights of children, birth parents, and adoptive parents. States have differed in their attempts to balance competing interests in this sensitive area of family relationships, and state laws vary accordingly. For this reason, although this chapter has highlighted some of the major legal issues, adoptive parents will need to rely on the advice of a competent and trusted attorney. Throughout this long and sometimes complicated legal process, parents need to be encouraged by remembering what a blessing it is to live in a society that respects the parent-child relationship and proceeds cautiously in establishing this intimate, lifelong commitment. When legal obstacles are encountered, we know that God remains in control: "The king's heart [or the judge's!] is in the hand of the LORD; he directs it like a watercourse wherever he pleases" (Prov. 21:1, NIV).

6

Welcoming a New Member

Current magazines carry many stories about "the lifestyle of the eighties." Most of the articles are talking about personal habits and a way of living that do not describe most Christians. Perhaps you are not "baby-boomers" or "two-professional" families and do not identify with current writing on lifestyle. Whether or not the way you live is pictured in those articles, you should remember that everyone has a lifestyle. We each have ways in which we habitually do things. We have a schedule, sometimes more or less rigid. We have spending habits, health habits, and recreation habits. Each of us has a number of roles we fulfill in our family life. In our family Don handles the finances since it "depresses" Evelyn to pay bills, even when there is enough money in the account! On the other hand, Evelyn plans the shopping, including a once-a-month large grocery order. These types of small and large habitual ways of behaving constitute a lifestyle.

Changes in a Family

Some authors compare the family to a mobile, with each family member represented by a figure hanging from a thread attached to a central hanging core. You have seen such mobiles hanging over a crib for a baby to watch or as wind chimes hanging on a porch. The fascination of a mobile is that when one piece is moved, it has an effect on all the other parts. The figures of the chime swing and touch other figures, and each is designed to sound a different note. The result is planned to be pleasant, but it produces change and movement all through the mobile.

When a new member is added to a family or a member is taken away, it produces ripples in the family. The mobile is temporarily out of balance, and figures will bump against each other until a new balance is reached. The results of this type of change can be dramatic or subtle. The changes can produce some new and pleasant notes like the wind chimes, or an explosion like atoms bumping together and pushing apart. You cannot always anticipate what the nature or extent of change will be when you add a new member to your family, but you can be sure that changes *will* take place.

Characteristics of Change Situations

Although each family member may have some unique way of adapting to change, there are some general reactions to change that could be called typical. Each of us can think of change times when we have reacted in one or more of the following ways:

Increased anxiety. Change usually makes us anxious. We are used to a uniform way of handling many of the routine matters of life, and when these routines are disrupted it makes us upset. Usually we can establish a satisfactory alternate routine, but we frequently feel uneasy while we are doing it. When we are anxious we are usually worried, without a clear thing to worry about. We are often more irritable. We frequently have difficulty sleeping. Since anxiety is a common reaction to change, we should not be surprised and should be prepared for it.

Increased emotionality. Anticipation of actual adoption produces intense emotions, especially joy. For many families the adoption is the end of a long series of delays, heightened emotionally by the strong desire to have a child. For other families the adoption comes at the end of an intense inner struggle. Should we raise this child? Is it the right thing to do? For others the adoption is the climax of a long period of legal hassling to free the child for adoption. Whatever the situation, this charged-up emotionality in looking forward to the adoption will affect your ability to adapt to change. Once the child is taken into the family, there are three possible emotional reactions you should be aware of.

The first is an up-and-down feeling. All of us have had emotional highs. We are so happy we feel as if we are going to burst, or so thankful that we can hardly stop expressing it. However, none of us has the energy or emotional drive to live continually on an emotional peak, whether it is joy over a new child or a mountaintop spiritual experience at a summer conference. Many times the return to an ordinary emotional state feels like a letdown. What should be normal is felt as mediocre.

A second important emotional reaction to change is depression. Some of us react to any highly emotional situation with sadness and depression. We may express this with crying or excessive sleeping. If we often cry for no apparent reason and have difficulty stopping, and crying is accompanied by continual sad feelings, we should beware.

Some of us do not react to changing situations with depression or sadness or tearfulness. Instead we may feel like striking out at something or someone. Anger is the third common emotional reaction. Angry outbursts are more common to males, and tearfulness to women, but this is not always the case. At times men feel like crying and cover it with a sullen withdrawal, or women feel like an angry outburst but hide their feelings with steely politeness.

Reactions of anxiety and general emotionality are not only likely in parents but also in the child who is being adopted and in siblings in the adopting home. They, too, may be frightened or letdown or depressed or angry or weepy! Many reactions of children, especially older children, when they first come into your home may not predict their long-term behavior. We have had foster children who were angels before chaos broke loose, and other children who had a tough time initially and then settled down. My favorite illustration is our younger son, who would not smile at Don for the first two weeks and turned out to be one of the most pleasant, smiling, delightful children we have known.

Learning opportunities. One of the encouraging characteristics of change situations is the opportunity for learning. Someone has said that a rut is a grave with both ends kicked out. That may be a little too graphic, but all of us find that we want things the way they were. It may not be the best, but it feels comfortable and we tend to resist change. Even when we have looked forward to change, we may find that the reality of the situation is different from the dream we had of how things would be. When we do not like the new situation, we frequently switch to idealizing the past and forget its own less-than-perfect realities. The adopted older child might begin to talk in glowing terms of the foster home or institution he previously could not stand. Or new parents may remember only the good parts of the situation in the years B.C. (Before Child!).

Part of the process of pregnancy is the growing reality that pregnancy is not always pleasant. The woman who is heavy, who has a back that hurts, who cannot sleep at night, and who frequently feels tired and unattractive is likely to find great relief in the arrival of the baby. The remembered circumstances of pregnancy make it difficult to think that "everything was great before the baby arrived and disrupted schedules [etc.]." The termination of the pregnancy discomfort helps to compensate for feelings of being overwhelmed by the new baby. The adopting parent does not usually have a nine-month preparation that is characterized by growing physical discomfort to help balance the onset of changes and problems of new parenthood.

All of the changes and reactions to change are not necessarily negative. Changes can also bring joy, relief, and excitement. These are the reactions that need to be maximized.

Techniques for Handling Change

It is not enough to know what the reactions to change are likely to be or even to recognize these reactions when they occur. What is needed are techniques for handling change. Some of the following techniques may prove helpful:

Awareness. One of the most important techniques for handling change is awareness. Frequently we react in emotional ways to situations without actually thinking about or planning those actions. Unless we develop methods or habits to make ourselves aware of what it is we are responding to and what it is we are feeling, it is unlikely that we will be able to get control of our responses. When our children were growing up, they pointed out to Dad that he usually ended up hollering at one of them when we packed the car for a trip. He became aware that he was tense and anxious as we packed and then tried to determine what *specifically* made him upset about packing. Next he learned to control his behavior and be relaxed in getting ready for a trip.

One specific thing you might do in making yourself aware is to go back to the mapping exercise in chapter 2. You were asked to make a list of changes you anticipated the adoption would bring. Now go back and check the list. Which changes actually happened? How did you react to the changes? What changes happened that you did not anticipate? It would be helpful if you and your spouse and siblings could do this together. One of the things you should try to do as part of this exercise is to clarify your emotions. If you cried, were you feeling joy, anger, or depression? If Dad hollered at the kids, was he feeling anger, anxiety, or desperation? This type of awareness and clarifying of your own emotions will help you in correctly interpreting the emotions of an older adopted new member of the family. Many times we get angry when we are scared. Frequently we act bored when we are really anxious. We sometimes cry when we are very angry. Children do the same things, and it helps to be able to clarify with them what the emotional expression indicates about feelings.

Maximize good continuity. A second technique for handling change is to maximize good continuity in the life of the child. Children, other than newborns, have habits, belongings, and a

personal self that need to be maintained. While it may seem like a
treat to go out and buy a new child a whole new wardrobe, a new
set of toys, and other personal things like toothbrush, blankets,
and pillows, the new should be incorporated with the old. A ratty
old toy feels like it belongs and provides continuity with the past.
We have been amazed at how some children manage to hang on
to a toy or a pillow or a blanket or a shirt long after they would
have been thrown away under normal circumstances. Belongings
frequently provide a point of stability. Even though parents may
change and place of abode changes, the child needs some continuity and some symbols of that continuity. Another important
point of continuity is a child's first name. One measure of self-
esteem is how a child feels about his name, because a name
comes to signify "me." Sometimes parents want to name the new
member of the family. With a very young child (under six months
of age), this is an opportunity to emphasize membership in the
family. If other siblings have been named after aunts or uncles or
other relatives, the new baby also will know that his name was
chosen in the same way. With an older child, who has already
learned to respond to a name, the task of incorporation by
naming is more difficult. To simply rename the child is bound to
cause confusion and takes away an important aspect of continuity. Some families have used the middle name as a bridge between the past and the future. Giving a new middle name allows
continuity and the possibility of change. You can use both names
and gradually switch to calling the child by the middle name.
You can add a name that is after someone in the new family. We
know one family with a birth son and three adopted sons who
have used the father's middle name for the middle name of all
four sons.

The second major aspect of continuity involves the continuity
of the adopting family and integrating the new member into that
continuity. Change and continuity work against each other. The
greater the change, the less continuity—and vice versa. The task
facing the adopting parents is to adjust to change while preserv-
ing continuity and integrating the new member into that stream.

One important aspect of continuity is built around meals and bedtime. A set mealtime that is attended by all family members is a terrific force for continuity. Work and school schedules vary, and in every family there will be occasional absences, but if the expectation is that *all* family members eat meals together unless there is a good reason for being absent, the family adjusts quickly. Mealtime can then provide a time of continuity. In our family we connected a short family worship time with breakfast and read a continuing story after dinner. One of the questions at dinner among the kids was: "What did you do today?"

Bedtimes also provide a time for ritual and continuity. Singing, short games, and story time all provide "something we always do in our family." Other traditions add notes of continuity: Saturday breakfast out or at home cooked by Dad and the kids; celebrating birthdays in particular ways; family scrapbooks to which the new child's picture and history are added. When the new child comes into the family, efforts need to be made to help the newcomer fit into traditional ways of doing things and to incorporate some of his ways of doing things into the family traditions.

The church also provides a source of continuity. "We always go to church" is a type of continuity. In addition the church provides different rituals that can help the new child to be integrated into the family. A baptism or dedication ceremony is a sign that this child is a member of a family that is claiming God's promises to children of believers and makes a strong public statement about this permanent addition to your family. Teaching of other ritual or traditional church practices such as the closing hymn, the creed to be recited, the physical motions (standing, hands upraised, kneeling)—and when these will happen in the service—will help the child feel that he knows what is going on and is a part of the congregation. Prepare an older child for the service by explaining what will happen and what is expected of him. After the service, talk about what the child did not understand. This will help the newcomer to more quickly feel at home. Each of us is so used to what happens at church that we can easily forget that it will be new and strange to someone who has not had our experiences.

Practical techniques. There are many practical techniques for adapting to changes in your life. Two of them are "time-out periods" and extra help. We often arrange these for mothers who have given birth to a baby. Friends will say, "It is time you new parents had a night out; let me watch the baby." Our daughter lives next to her in-laws, and they have had a practice of taking their grandson for an hour most evenings so that the parents can have some time alone. This time of temporary retreat from the pressures of parenthood has been a blessing. Evelyn and I started getting up a half-hour earlier each weekday, making coffee in our room, reading Scripture, and simply talking about problems, blessings and what the plans for the day are. We usually close our time in prayer. This quiet time has been a blessing, and we would urge you to establish some time when you and your spouse can be alone together.

Extra physical help is often provided after childbirth. Evelyn has gone to each of our children's homes to help with the new baby. The physical labor of caring for an infant tends to add to other pressures of parenthood. Friends and relatives recognize this. Part of the outpouring of help is because of the physical recovery necessary after pregnancy. When an adoption takes place, it would be well if you, Mother, were treated as if you just had a new baby. If possible, you should have some housecleaning help. Recently I heard a neat idea. A Sunday-school class gives new mothers a day of housework from each member as a present! Diaper service is often a gift at baby showers. All of these things will help the new adopting parent, too, and you should gratefully accept any good-intentioned offers of assistance.

General principles. We will close this section with two general principles to help manage change. First, when you are going to welcome a new member into your family, try to arrange the timing to minimize other changes. Adopting a new family member adds great family stress, as does a family move or a job change or a major illness of a family member. Other occasions of major stress are family members leaving for college or the armed services. The general rule should be that one major change at a time is enough stress for the family to handle! You may not be able to arrange life events as you would desire, but awareness of potential stress events may help in your planning.

The second principle is to approach adoption with a deep-rooted sense of God's providence. You are responsible for making wise decisions, but God is in charge. You need to relax in the confidence that God has promised to make all things work together for good to those who love him and are called according to his purposes (Rom. 8:28). A plaque hangs in Don's office that Evelyn gave him during a series of family trials. We were facing a new career, some of our children were having serious problems, and things in general were not going well. The plaque is inscribed:

> Out of darkness shall come dawn.
> Out of winter shall come spring.
> Out of striving shall come peace.
> Not by our power but by the power of God.

Remembering that peace and dawn and spring come by the power of God can give us a sense of continuity that holds us up during times of change and difficulty.

Common Problems Adopting Parents Face

In preparation for this book, we surveyed a group of adoptive parents. One question we asked was, "What problems did you experience in the first months of having the new child as a member of the family?" We would like you to know some of the more frequent problems mentioned. (In this chapter we are dealing with transient problems of the first few weeks. Similar difficulties which may persist or deepen are covered in chapter 7, "Big and Little Failures.")

Physical Ailments

One of the most frequently mentioned difficulties during the early weeks were colds and other related infections such as eyes, ears, nose, and throat. Children often come down with colds when they move into foster care or change homes. The receiving family also frequently reacts with colds. This may be due to the stress associated with change. Or it may be because the child and family expose each other to new sets of germs to which they have not acquired resistance. Whatever the reason, it is harder to get used to each other if nobody is feeling quite up to par. On the other hand, minor sicknesses provide a good opportunity to show love and concern and tenderness in a practical way. You can be prepared by having standard cold remedies on hand and an emergency number for your family doctor. With young babies, colic is not unusual. If the newborn is up most of the night, parents may need some extra help during the day.

Schedule Adjustments

Families also mentioned the schedule adjustments that had to do with including another person in the couple's lifestyle. These problems are similar to those of first-time parents in birth families. The phrase "a baby makes all the difference in the world" may be an exaggeration, but a baby certainly makes a world of difference in the life of a couple. Adopting parents mentioned that a baby's wakefulness at night made it hard to get enough sleep. They mentioned the lack of time alone or alone together. Family free time was squeezed out. Some of this was due to the new baby's schedule and demands, but some of the time crunch was caused by visits from relatives, friends, and other interested persons. All of us want our new baby to be noticed but, when overdone, other people can make you tired, simply by being there. The major burden of caring for a baby typically falls on the mother of the house. The father may have to help set limits and see that friends and family realize she needs to be treated with the consideration given any new mother.

New Relationships

Difficulty with establishing new relationships was mentioned by parents who had adopted older children, especially if there was a communication barrier. If the child spoke a foreign language, both parents and child had to learn to communicate around a language that was strange to each. Other difficulties

seem to depend on previously learned techniques and communication patterns. Many children who are adopted at an older age
have experienced much trauma. They have frequently learned to
deal with harsh situations in ways that are not helpful in normal
family life. Lying, manipulation, or temper tantrums may all have
been effective coping devices for a child previously abused or
moved from one set of adults to another. But these methods are
destructive to normal family life. It will help if you can approach
this as a learning opportunity. For example: lying is a moral
problem, but the child who lies needs to learn that falsehood is
wrong and also needs to learn how to respond truthfully. He
needs to learn that the truth works in family life.

Another aspect that occasionally causes difficulties in establishing a new relationship are the prior bonds of the children. The
desire to be with someone else can hinder establishing a new
relationship. The child who feels that to accept you as parents
means he has to give up loving his birth parents or a foster parent
is in a terrible emotional bind. All children need to learn that
love is not a finite commodity and that they may love two people
at once.

Siblings

The major problem parents mentioned in relation to siblings is
how to help other children in the family understand, deal with,
and not imitate the behavior problems of the new child. This
problem is generally most acute with adolescents, and an ounce
of prevention may be worth a pound of cure. Our experience
leads us to urge you strongly not to add foster or adopted
adolescents to your family if it already includes adolescents.
Under special circumstances this may be necessary, but the
possibilities and frequency of unhappy or tragic outcomes are
high. We also caution you about taking an adopted child who will
be the oldest of an already established sibling group. The oldest
child in a family has some rights of leadership and responsibility.
To replace the oldest may provide a new and uncertain model
who will have automatic status due to age. It is also likely to cause

resentment in the child being replaced. Usually the ideal situation is for the new child to be the youngest member of the family. This is not always possible. Many older children need homes, and agencies frequently make less-than-desirable placements because of the press of the situation, but you should be cautious and discuss this concept very carefully with your social worker. Age position is an important developmental aspect of children.

Family Advice

Family interference, advice giving, and some "you did not consult us, so sink or swim" attitudes were mentioned as problems. Although some of these would also be present with pregnancy and birth, they seem to be especially difficult for adopting parents. Perhaps this is because adoption involves a series of public decisions, and it is normal to need bolstering to confirm that you were right in your choices and can do the job you have chosen. Ordinary comments and criticism may strain your confidence. Contact with other adopting parents can serve as a source of encouragement if that support is not coming from relatives. As they have become more aware of this potential problem, some agencies have begun to add one or more relatives or close friends to the adoption process by inviting them to adoptive group meetings or presentations of the child—with consent of the adopting family, of course.

Sense of Responsibility

Couples usually have an increased sense of responsibility when they become natural parents. The same thing happens to adopting parents, particularly if it is a first child. There *is* less freedom. The man with a family cannot change jobs as easily. The woman can make few choices without considering the baby. This increased responsibility, coupled with the unfamiliarity of parenting, does constitute a weight for some couples. Time spent with other parents and a conscious concentration on the blessings of each day help to lift some of the burden.

Bedtime

One problem mentioned by adopting parents was a set of bedtime annoyances. Crying, stalling, fear of being alone, and getting back out of bed were all mentioned. Both ritual and flexibility are needed. A night light will help conquer childhood fears. Bedtime stories and a set ritual that ends with bed will help form new habits. Consistency is crucial in putting the child back in bed when he gets up. Habits are established and re-formed by consistency; if the child is sometimes successful in getting out and joining in activities, he will be justly confused and will not unlearn a bad habit. Most child-care books have good suggestions for handling bedtime problems.

Privacy Issues

A number of adopting families mentioned a range of minor problems that all have to do with privacy. Some found that with a newly adopted child, things that were previously private were no longer so. One said, "I have found it hard to adjust to the fact that nothing in our home is off-limits to the new child. He gets into everything!" Another issue of privacy is the personal, probing questions by friends and relatives. Most likely Ann Landers would say, "Look them in the eye and ask, 'Why would you want to know that?'" But many of us find it difficult to deal with well-meaning but insensitive friends and relatives in that manner. You should think of such stock answers as "We have decided not to share with anyone some of the background information" or "The agency has advised us not to share much of the information we have." If you are ready for most questions, they will not catch you off-guard.

There is also need for privacy within the family. You should have privacy for yourself and some of your things. It is appropriate, for example, that a desk or chest be off-limits or that children ask permission before coming into your bedroom. Children also need privacy. As a general rule you should not read children's letters or listen in on their phone conversations. If you suspect that things are happening you should know about, you should ask; and if you plan to check up on your children, you should tell them. Each of us needs a part of ourselves that we reserve the right to share or not to share. It is only when sharing is voluntary that it is an act of giving and trusting.

Feelings Follow Behavior

Frequently we act on the principle that we must know before we do, or that we must feel right about people before we can act in right ways toward them. The scriptural principle is that we do what God commands—and *then* we know. If we act in godly ways, the right feelings will follow. When you take a new member into your family, all of the "right" emotions are not necessarily present. You have to learn to love and cherish each other, and this takes time, especially with older children. Go ahead and *act* in loving ways. Treat the child as if you had all of the feelings you would like to have, and you will begin to develop those feelings.

Adjusting to a new family member is not always easy, but it does have great rewards. One adopted teenager said that when he was studying genetics, he was trying to figure out why he had brown eyes. His mother said, "Well, your father has brown eyes," to which he replied, "But, Mom, I was adopted." His mother looked at him and said, "I know, but unless I really think about it, I just forget that fact." May something similar happen to all of us who have the joy of adopting.

7

Important Questions Children Ask

Sue stood in the kitchen a little apprehensively. Finally she said, "You know, Mom, I think I am a worthwhile person." Her mother looked at her sharply and said, "Well, if you are so worthwhile, why don't you empty the garbage instead of leaving your jobs for someone else to do!"

Many of you may think that it would be the rare parent who would treat a teenager so harshly, but that is not the case. A teacher who was working on developing a high-school course on self-concept gave as a typical assignment the saying of "I am a worthwhile person" to a family member. Of an approximate 125 students who completed the assignment, only one student reported that she received a wholehearted, positive response from that family member. This was a young girl whose mother said, "Jane, your father and I have always strongly felt that you were worthwhile and are really worth an awful lot to us."

Worth, belonging, competence, and meaning are ideas that seem to crowd in upon us at crucial times in our lives. These ideas raise key questions for all of us. Whether we are born into a family or adopted, we must struggle to understand: Who am I? Where do I belong? What can I do? What am I worth? Knowing answers to these questions seems to be especially important to adolescents. Young children usually have only a few questions about these central issues of life. Suddenly, with adolescence, many come storming to the surface.

Answering these questions is never easy, but the answers have added dimensions of difficulty for the adopted child. Answers to the basic questions raise a whole series of related questions that most of us do not have to face because they do not apply to us. Why was I given up? Was I not wanted? Do I really fit in this family? Trying to answer these related questions may block attention to the basic issues.

All persons must arrive at a settled, confident view of themselves and their place in the world on the basis of a positive sense of belonging, competence, and worth. As these self-referent ideas are integrated to our satisfaction, we have freedom to see the meaning of life and our place in life. No other person can give us these positive ideas of self. We have to find an answer for ourselves, and to some extent it is a lifelong task. But we can help each other deal with the questions raised and help each other come to answers based on knowing God and his Word.

God has given us a basis for knowing who we are, why we are here, and what we should be doing while we are here. The Trinity has special relevance to these questions. God the Father teaches us where we belong. Christ the Son teaches us that we have worth. The Holy Spirit teaches us that we are competent because he gives us his gifts. As we examine the questions of life in detail, our relationship to God becomes central.

Who Am I?

This is the basic question, and it has one basic answer. We are children of God through the Lord Jesus Christ. All other aspects of our being should be filtered through the fact that God has made us in his image, he has called us through his Son, and he is in the process of fitting us to spend eternity with him by making us like his Son. Each of us will find there are things about ourselves we do not like and that we wish were different. But our acceptance of ourselves does not depend on liking everything about ourselves. It rests on being children of God and precious in his sight.

Each of us, as we come to know ourselves, will have to deal with what we have been given. The child of God has been given a physical body, a mind, and a personality.

"I Am a Person with a Body"

None of us has a strictly accurate view of our body. We tend to see our physical self as we used to be or as we would like to be. We may see our body as worse or better than it really looks to others. Rare is the adolescent who is satisfied with his appearance! Adults have learned how to view themselves by a history of comparison and evaluation. Most of us come to terms with the fact that no one has a perfect body, and we would probably not trade our disliked aspects for whatever it is that someone else doesn't like about his body. It is enlightening to hear some of the things that people don't like about themselves. They often don't like their weight. Disliked noses also seem to rank high. Others would like to change sweaty hands or long necks. When you talk with people about what they dislike about themselves physically, it frequently does not turn out to be what you would expect. Our self-perceptions are really that—perceptions. They represent not objective physical features but how the person sees those features. This happens with each of us in relation to ourselves and also in relation to others. How frequently you see the beauty in persons only as you begin to love them!

The adopted child has a special problem with physical self-perceptions. He does not share the genetic background of the adoptive parents and siblings. Sometimes there are distinct differences in general characteristics. Ordinarily we look to parents and older siblings to learn what is "beautiful." The adopted child who has different features and characteristics from the rest of the family does not have this advantage. This means that parents must go out of their way to point out the beauty of the child and the characteristics to be admired about himself.

One of our adopted children, who has beautiful brown eyes, is the only brown-eyed person in the family. We made up words for a nighttime lullaby for each of our children. A personalized version of "Beautiful, Beautiful Brown Eyes" became his special song. One time a waitress in a strange restaurant asked persistent questions about this brown-eyed child in a blue-eyed family. The children chose to enjoy her puzzlement rather than explain that their little brother was adopted, and he enjoyed the special attention. Back in the car a few minutes later, all four children were singing "Beautiful Brown Eyes" together. Our son learned to look upon brown eyes as a badge of beauty and distinction.

"I Am Also a Person with a Mind"

Being created in the image of God means that we have been given a rational nature. We can think. We can reason. We can know right and wrong and make choices. Our society puts great emphasis on intellectual skills, but it is unfortunate that much of this emphasis is focused on the intellectual skills necessary in school. Although school skills are not necessarily those that will be needed later in life, they are the ones that are used to judge a child's intellectual ability. While there is much debate about how much of this ability is inherited as opposed to learned, it is almost universally agreed that some aspects are inherited. By and large, children are like their parents, but some of this is genetic and some of it is learned as the child grows up with the parents teaching him. Adopted children, particularly children who are adopted when they are older, face special problems in coming to know what their intellectual abilities are.

One evening our fifth-grade son was riding in the car with us on the way to see his sister play volleyball. Without preliminary, he suddenly asked, "Did my first parents graduate from high school?" We answered that we were pretty sure they did, talked a bit about them, and then asked, "What made you wonder that?" His answer was: "Well, our principal said at assembly today that all of us kids had smart parents and there was just no excuse if we didn't do good work. And I've just been having so much trouble that I wondered about my birth parents." A broad, encouraging generalization from the principal raised genetic questions for our adopted son.

There is another problem. In most cases children who come into adoption later than newborn are behind in learning skills. This deficit is usually due to the family stress and turmoil that preceded the adoption. It is almost impossible for children to focus attention needed for academic learning if they are in high stress and turmoil at home. Consequently they fall behind. The greatest danger in falling behind is the labeling that sometimes accompanies it. "Who am I?" can get answered with "I am a dummy." When that happens, the child usually falls further behind. Recently I heard a professor in special education say, "Most kids who are classified as 'learning disabled' can do very well outside of rigid school education. The only thing the label 'learning disabled' means is that the schools don't know how to teach the child and it is easier to blame it on the child." He went on to say that the number-one thing needed for kids who are having trouble in school is the experience of success. At times we can arrange success by helping the child catch up. At other times the success must be provided outside of school. It is extremely important that the answer to "Who am I?" with respect to intellectual ability is not entirely based on how well the child is able to perform in the school situation.

"I Am a Person with Feelings"

Feelings are important. Feelings alone are not a good basis for actions, but we should not go to the other extreme of giving the impression that they are not important. We should remember that when Christ was asked what the greatest commandment was, he said, "Thou shalt love. . . ." First of all the Lord, and then our neighbor. While love has an action dimension, it also is something that should be loaded with feelings. It is difficult to read the Psalms without being touched with the outpouring of feelings. As children of God we are to have feelings. We need to acknowledge them and to use them in service.

For a number of reasons, your adopted child may have difficulty identifying and acknowledging feelings. Some children who
come into adoption or foster care have learned to suppress their
feelings. Perhaps they were trying to protect a childlike parent.
Perhaps expressing feelings led to abusive punishment. Sometimes a different cultural background defined correct public expression of feeling in a different way. Parents who adopt older
children must be patient and sensitive to the way the new child
does or does not express feelings. It is very important that other
members of the family model having feelings, expressing them,
and acting on them in suitable ways.

In addition to seeing that you have feelings, your children will
need help in identifying and putting into words what they are
feeling. Talking is one way of coming to understand. You can say,
"I know that it hurts when we talk about this." "I know that I would
feel this. . . ." Recently our daughter Ruth was working with a
young boy who had not been told he was adopted until he was
eleven. Shortly after being told, he began a whole series of
destructive actions at school. She told us she looked over his
record before meeting with him and tried to think about how she
would feel at twelve if someone had kept something as important
as being adopted from her and then dumped it on her. When she
met with the boy, she said, "You really have been goofing off at
school. Sounds like you are really mad at someone. I notice that
your folks did not tell you that you were adopted until last month.
I have an adopted brother, and I know he would be mad as hops if
my folks had kept something as important as that a secret from
him. I think you are really mad at your parents, and I can understand why." The boy looked at her as though someone had
turned on a switch and they spent about an hour talking about
how he felt, reasons why his folks had done what they did, and
how important forgiveness is to a family. Refusing or neglecting to
talk about feelings seldom means that the feelings have gone
away. It usually means that the feelings are underground and
having an effect, but the child does not have the tools of language
to help him understand and control them.

The answer to the question "Who am I?" lays groundwork for answering other important questions.

Where Do I Belong?

Where one belongs is a complicated question for all of us, partly because "belonging" includes a wide range of meaning. It has special meaning for adopted children.

In our house we sometimes ask "Who belongs to these shoes?" especially if they are in the middle of the floor. The question acknowledges that belonging has to do with owning and taking responsibility. For the adopted child, "Where do I belong?" means belonging to someone and having things that belong to him.

Sometimes we say, "You may not use that. It belongs to me." Then we are saying that belonging implies possession and control. The adopted child wonders, "Does this family I live with have possession and control of me? Or should my biological parents have me?"

Our children visited various colleges before they made their choices. Several times we heard: "I just don't feel like I could belong there." Belonging has to do with feeling we are in a place suitable for us. Recently our academically tired son said, "I guess I just don't belong in this family—all my sisters got A's easily." We didn't leave the subject there, of course, because suitable fit has many dimensions that together add to a sense of belonging.

Knowing that we are connected, that we are in the right place, that we possess and are possessed, are all part of belonging and provide answers to "Where do I belong?" In its most basic form, the answer to that question is "Where God puts me"! But it is not easy to come to a realization and acceptance of this answer. Children watch us struggle with why we are working where we are, why we are living where we are, whom we accept as our connections, and who rejects us. As they watch us they see us struggling with those lifelong questions. Recently I have thought of Moses. In forty desert years he must have asked himself frequently, "Do I belong in Egypt? My family, the work I was trained to do, and the culture where I am at home are there. What am I doing in the desert?" It is clear from Scripture that the only satisfying answer Moses could give was "I am here because God put me here!" If the basic answer is "I belong where God puts me," this should help us deal with some related questions.

Being adopted seems to make the answer to the question of belonging much more difficult. Some of the factors we use to determine where we belong may not be present for the adopted child. The fact that I look like my parents or another family member tells me I belong. The fact that I have pictures of the family that include me tells me I belong. The whole history of the family together reminds me that I have a common experience and that I belong. For the adopted child, these things are often missing. It is frequently helpful to the child to construct a history of his belonging.

For example, we kept a baby book for each of the children born to us. We made a special effort to create a similar book for our adopted sons. Since we had no baby pictures, their books began with their arrival in our family. There are pictures of the extended family with the newest son in the lap of the oldest cousin. There is a picture of Grandmother Felker holding Jeff after his first haircut and Donny decked out in the first outfit Mother made for him. We made conscious choices to picture our children in inclusive ways. When the old albums come out, as they frequently do, no child feels left out.

Into the book also went pictures taken on adoption day. The courthouse and the judge fill the role of doctor and hospital. Our whole family (including the other children) went to court to witness the adoptions, and rare restaurant meals celebrated the occasions in style. Family ritual, family pictures, and telling the family story to include the adoption can all contribute to building the historical sense of belonging.

At times it is possible to obtain some pre-adoption history for the child. Photographs, birth records, health records, and prior school achievements all provide sources that can be incorporated into an individual history and can contribute to a sense of belonging. Although you may fear that such a history would tie the child to his former life and make it difficult for him to feel a part of the present family, our own experience does not confirm such fears. A sense of who I am and how I got to where I am provides a basis for a sense of belonging.

Do these things work? For many months after his adoption, our older son told anyone who would listen: "Uncle Don is my daddy, Aunt Evelyn is my mother now." Jeff introduced his four-year-old self for weeks with "I'm Jeffrey William Felker, adopted boy." He always commented when we passed the courthouse or heard the name of "his" judge on the news. Of course, belonging is an ongoing struggle for everyone but the foundations can be laid and accepted.

For the adopted child, there are two possible situations that will require extra thought about belonging. One is abandonment and the other is dual parents. Some children come into adoption because they were abandoned by their parents. Others enter the adoption process because one or both birth parents cooperated to make this plan out of love and responsibility. Regardless of which happened in a particular situation, the adopted child is likely to ask, "Why was I not wanted?" In the eyes of the child he was unwanted and given away. The child's adopted parents and others must help him handle the facts of his birth and relinquishment. When possible and suitable, an explanation of the parent's choice should be given. You may know facts about the motivations of the parent that can reassure the child that he was loved and wanted and that what was done was for his good and out of love. The Bible tells us that God gave his only begotten Son out of love. Giving that involves pain can be a sign of love—and if this is the case, the child needs that reassurance. It is also important that the child realize that none of us totally chooses where we will be. We are all dependent upon the Lord to place us somewhere; for the adopted child, this is another way God has chosen to bring together a family.

The dual family brings a different type of problem, related to the question of: "How do I love two sets of parents?" Some adopted children need our permission to love two sets of parents. It is a difficult thing for many parents to give that permission. I have thought frequently that one of the joys of marriage is that I now have another family to love and be loved by. When I married I received a second set of parents and have learned to love them. Loving my in-laws has not taken away from my love for my parents; it has enlarged my life. As an adoptive parent I have found it reassuring to know that my adopted children can love and think about and know about their biological parents and that it need not detract from their love for me. Adopted children have told us how much more they love their adoptive parents because they willingly permitted them to love their other parents, too.

In dealing with the concept of belonging, our adopted children have found it helpful that there are other children in our family circle who are also adopted. Our sister's family has three adopted children, our brother's family has two adopted children, we have two adopted children. Many of our friends have adopted children. This has helped all of the children to see that adopted children are loved, that they *do* fit, and therefore they can fit, too! While we might think that our children would know this from the way we treat them, it is sometimes easier for children to look objectively at others. Friends who are adopted can also provide a support group. One of our sons was struggling with his adoption in relation to a job move. He felt that if he had not been adopted, he would not have had to move and give up all his friends at the old place. He was also anxious about finding new friends. When we got to the new place, his first friend turned out to be adopted, too. It was a relief to our son to realize that every place has adopted kids and that being adopted doesn't guarantee either staying or moving! In addition to other problems, making a secret of adoption works against developing supports for the child.

What Can I Do?

For Christians, vocational choice—what can I do?—breaks down into two main questions. What gifts has God given me? How can I use them to serve him? Like life's other important questions, the answers are never final. We change and develop during our whole lifetime, and the answers to basic questions take on new dimensions and meaning as we change.

Along with other adolescents, the adopted child hits upon this question with special force in the teenage years. People begin to ask him: "Where are you going to college?" "What do you plan to do after high school?" "Do you have a part-time job yet?" "Are you going into your dad's business [farm, store, profession, etc.]?" Boys and girls alike are expected to choose a life work and begin preparing in earnest for it during the adolescent years. They need our help but sometimes have trouble asking for it. While we parents may want to phrase the question in Christian terms, they may be very shy about talking "religion" and reluctant to give God control of this aspect of their lives. How we are handling and have handled our own gifts and vocation will be more effective guidance than specific teaching at this point. We can also offer indirect support in other ways.

Adolescents will be concerned with figuring out what they can do well enough to earn a living and often have unrealistically low ideas of their own abilities. Because the focus at school is on a limited range of skills, a child who does not do well in school may mistakenly believe he is incompetent. I heard a thirteen-year-old say as he contemplated his dismal report card, "Mother, am I average at anything?" I knew the child well enough to know that he was far above average in social skills, very well coordinated physically, and had an extremely strong and healthy body. In the conversation that followed, it was clear that he knew these things about himself but did not know that they would help him find and do well in a job. He had been worrying a great deal about finding work, since he was seeing daily newspaper stories about unemployment.

On the other hand, sometimes parents tell us they are worried that their adolescent seems to have an inflated idea of the kind of vocational choice he can succeed in, considering his present work habits or abilities. Since a great deal of maturation will take place in the adolescent years, and our society provides many opportunities for returning to school or retraining, it is neither necessary nor wise to discourage aspirations beyond the child's present performance or competence. Naturally, you do not want your child to fail, but perhaps God plans to teach something important by that route. Some of the steps outlined later in this section may help the child set more realistic goals or realize that more effort will be needed to reach higher ones.

Another aspect of "What can I do?" involves coming to terms with disabilities. Some children who apparently adjusted well to chronic conditions like diabetes, to permanent disability such as loss of a limb, or to other physical limitations appear to go into a tailspin during adolescence. One reason may be the realization that the condition they have experienced as children will continue, and their surging need for independence comes up against the reality that they are limited in their adult choices. These adolescents can be helped to realize that every person has some disability. Some are more visible than others, and some invisible ones are much more limiting than those your child shows to the world. If the need to feel competent is bumping hard against the fact of a disability, your adolescent may need some short-term counseling from a person competent to help. The young person needs an answer to the question "Why did God make me like this?"

In talking with young people, it is easy to focus on lacks and limitations, as we try to help them arrive at a vocation by a process of elimination. This is especially likely to happen if the adolescent has not formed a strong idea of what he *would* like to try. It is important to remember that God has given each person gifts to use. It is our job to discover and appreciate them. Even when those gifts are not readily apparent, we can trust God. Jesus said, "Follow me and I will make you . . . ." We can encourage our children to follow Jesus and expect that he will keep his promise to make them useful servants.

Exposure to a wide variety of people is useful to young people who are trying to determine what they can do. Adopted children sometimes mistakenly feel that if they had biological parents, they would be like them and the question would be much simpler. Of course, that is not true, and all children need many adult role models. Exposure to a wide variety of people increases the opportunity to find an adult Christian who has some of the traits your child has and is happy and productive. Children also need exposure to a wide variety of jobs. If the wage earners in your family all work at offices, your children may not know anything about the life of a farmer or a factory worker. They may not know that some office workers stay at their desks most of the day and others drive all over the city making calls. Plan to let your children see men and women at work in all kinds of places at many different tasks. It will broaden vocational possibilities in their thinking.

It is important that your young person understand that all necessary work has dignity and value. I heard a college professor's wife expressing dismay that their son had matter-of-factly told them he was accepting a job with several negative factors "because the pay is great." I had heard many complaints from that family about the wage of college professors compared to steelworkers. The son had made a vocational choice on the basis of what he understood to be the way his family judged a job. Your children will notice if you consistently value all workers by the excellence of the job they do and the attitudes the worker takes toward that job. On the other hand, complaining about your own job while coveting the rewards of others is a sin that your children may imitate. It also says to the child "If you end up a steelworker [or whatever group you compare and complain about], I don't think you are as valuable as I am." What if your adopted child really wants to be a steelworker and not a college professor? It is important that our life and our words convey to our children the fact that all jobs are valuable and that gifts are given to be used.

Vocational choice is enormously wide for young people today. While this gives a sense of freedom and a high probability of a job to match every person's gifts and inclinations, it may also increase confusion and fear. The greatest help we can give our children in answering the question "What can I do?" is not advice. It is the demonstrated confidence that God has prepared them for work and will help them find and do it.

What Am I Worth?

We started this section with four important questions: *Who am I? Where do I belong? What can I do?* and *What am I worth?* The last question goes deeper than any other, and God has given an unequivocal answer. To him we are worth that which is most precious to him—the life of his Son. The ultimate measure of our worth is that loving act of sacrifice by the Triune God.

It is possible that your adopted child may struggle with questions of worth more than his friends, but this is not necessarily true. It depends on the circumstances of the adoption and on personality and style. Struggling or not, all children derive a sense of worth in the same ways.

You will want to teach them that God loves them unconditionally and sacrificially and pray for their response to that love. Please do not unintentionally teach them that God's love is based on their obedience or goodness. "If thou, oh LORD, shouldest mark iniquities . . . who shall stand?" certainly applies to children, too. Some children from Christian homes carry a great sense of unworthiness into adult life because they were taught and accepted the standards of the Word of God but did not learn how to accept forgiveness, restoration, and strength to live a life pleasing to God.

Children feel worth as they are loved, respected, and cared for by parents and others. They may lack a sense of worth when this is missing, either actually or in the child's perception. We are beginning to understand that even when a parent dies, children may blame themselves and feel they are somehow unworthy of parental love. The comments earlier about the circumstances of the child's relinquishment are important in connections with feelings of worth.

You demonstrate your children's worth as you are willing to sacrifice for their welfare. Of course, we do not mean to encourage a life of parental martyrdom. But it is important to realize that being parents will frequently require you to set aside your own comforts and desires and give to the child. The child is worth it!

Children feel worth as they see that what they give back to their parents is welcomed and brings joy. They need opportunities to give to us. They need to hear genuine expressions of our satisfaction in being their parents. Whether they bring us a grubby picture, a sticky bug, or an expensive tool that represents weeks of saving, each gift should be treasured because that communicates to the child that the giver has worth, too.

Who am I? Where do I belong? What can I do? What am I worth? Every person needs answers to these questions. Depending on their previous experiences, your adolescent adopted children may ask them with special urgency. By the grace of God, they will find answers adequate to move them on toward adulthood.

8

Big and Little Failures

Almost everyone knows firsthand of an adopted child who grew up unhappy and became a miserable adult. Others know of situations where the adoption didn't work at all and other arrangements were made. Since human beings tend to pass on these bad-news stories, there is a widespread feeling that adoption is a risky business. Somewhere in the back of your mind may be the thought "What if our adoption is one of the failures?"

Or perhaps you are reading this chapter because you are presently experiencing a sense of failure in your adoption experience. You are asking the question "Where did we go wrong?" Or "What do we do now?"

This chapter will approach the subject of failure at several different levels. We want you to have accurate information about adoption outcomes. There are some statistics and analyses available that may help put the myths in perspective and reassure you about the adoption process.

We also will discuss various kinds of failure within an individual adoption. Sometimes families need help with specific areas that are going poorly—the child is doing failing work in school or is persistently running away from home or getting involved in serious scrapes, or expected closeness is not developing in the family circle. There are many behaviors or groups of actions that can mar an adoption. There are also interventions and explanations that help in these situations.

Christians are vulnerable to a particular set of failure feelings, which may arise out of faulty teaching. The final section of this chapter will outline some spiritual traps that Christian adopting parents need to avoid. These traps may contribute to actual failures or lead to a false sense of guilt and failure.

Adoption Failure

One way to judge adoption success and adoption failure is to count the numbers. Various people have tried to do just that. Although their findings vary widely, this does not mean they are inaccurate. Rather, it probably reflects the fact that adoption practices vary, and judging whether an adoption outcome is successful depends on the assumptions with which you started. Writing in *Child Welfare* in March 1977, Alfred Kadushin summarized:

> . . . over the last ten years as a consequence of the work of the agencies, about 500,000 children were placed for adoption with parents who nurtured them and cared for them as their own. These were children who had lost, or never had, a home of their own. Many studies yield the same conclusion—that the failure rate during the first year of placement, as measured by the number of children returned to the agency is extremely low, 2% to 4%, and that 75% to 80% of the adopted children grew to healthy, satisfactory maturity in such homes.

The Spaulding agency for children, which offers adoption services to children many would classify as "unadoptable," has a disruption rate of approximately one in nine. Similar figures are quoted for other institutions that move older children from group-care situations to carefully selected and prepared adoptive homes. On the other hand, a small study in a state on the East Coast reported a disruption rate for older children of one in three.

Reasons for Disruption

As you consider these statistics and your own situation, how should you evaluate them? Let us begin by looking at the reasons for disruption. This is the word commonly used for an adoption situation where the child was actually placed in the home with the intent to complete an adoption, or where the adoption was actually completed, and at some later date the decision is made to discontinue or annul the process and the child is removed from the home.

Attachment failure. When experienced social workers listen carefully to families talking about disruption, the reason they most commonly hear from the adults is something like this: "The child just didn't become part of our family and didn't seem to want to." Workers categorize these as "failures of attachment." But while it is easy to see that this has happened, it is not easy to understand why. Parents will then go on to describe a list of behaviors that led them to believe the child did not want to be integrated into their family. But even while listening, an experienced social worker is aware that very similar behaviors and even more difficult ones have been met by other adopting families, and those families did not interpret the child's behaviors as rejection of the adopting family. How do families and children become convinced that they are not wanted by each other? Why does it happen? We don't really know. There are probably many different reasons.

Some adoptions disrupt because the child persistently and repeatedly makes it clear that he will not stay in the family. Adoptions arranged without the consent of older children may work out, but it is much safer to spend the time and energy to win the consent of the child to the adoption that is planned. Most children understand promises. If they have willingly given their word to try to become a part of a new family, they will work with parents and others who are trying to help them. All parties to older-child adoptions should be aware that children need to be convinced from the inside out that adoption is the route they should take. Trying to force adoption on an unwilling child is likely to hurt both family and child. If the child refuses adoption, other arrangements to meet the child's need for care and stability should be found.

Unrealistic expectations. Another factor that may contribute to disruption or to problems in becoming attached to each other involves unrealistic expectations. The myth of instant love is very widespread in our society. Not only are men and women supposed to be able to fall in love across a crowded room, it is also expected that parents and children will adore each other on contact. We are beginning to realize that this is not true even in biological parents and their newborn babies. Often there are many ambivalent feelings about becoming parents. Both mothers and fathers may become depressed, sad, or anxious as they contemplate what having the new baby means. With a little help from loving friends and relatives and some time to adjust, most parents learn to love and care for their new baby and may completely forget (if they ever admitted) that they were less than enthusiastic about the baby.

Adoption presents a similar situation, and the accompanying ambivalence may be even stronger. Generally, years of work and planning have gone into the placement of this child in the home. Parents have dreamed of this day but may now find themselves depressed by the reality of the child in the home. An older child may have a fantasy of "my very own family" that doesn't match at all with day-to-day living. In addition, society is unlikely to give permission to express any of these doubts. There is a wave of congratulations, gifts, excitement, and thanksgiving. How could a brand-new adopting parent in that situation say, "Hey, look, I don't feel all that great about this." Yet if they can be realistic about their feelings, especially to someone who can understand and respond with encouragement and help, it is more likely that the ambivalence will be replaced with bonding to the new child rather than harden into a feeling that the adoption was a mistake.

Too much, too soon. Disruptions may grow out of situations in which too much was expected too soon. The statistics quoted from Professor Kadushin cover adoptions made under conditions that no longer prevail—a period when the majority of placements were of white Anglo-Saxon infants in matching homes. Today's adoptions often bring together parents and children who have well-developed family histories. In many cases these children do not easily blend into their new families, and it may be years before the damage done by previous abuse, neglect, or multiple placements can be undone. In the genuine concern to find a home for every child, some workers may unintentionally minimize the effort and time that will be required before any response is seen in the child. Discouraged parents may come to feel that the depressing situation is somehow their fault and that the child could do better elsewhere, or that they just cannot go on without getting a response from a child. Follow-up support for older-child adoptions is an absolute necessity. Then families and workers can be sensitive to developing situations and offer help and encouragement before a minor problem deteriorates to the point of disruption. Adopting parents need to be prepared to accept slow change or even none at all. They need people to help them believe they are doing the best that can be done and that no one expects them to achieve overnight parenting success.

Poor preparation or matching. Sometimes adoptions disrupt because the child has been poorly prepared or the adoption worker did not know the child or the family well enough to arrange an adequate match between the family and the child. For example, one Anglo-Saxon family had expressed a willingness to take a child of any race. They had already successfully adopted two Oriental children. A new social worker read the old home study, visited once, and then arranged an adoption of a Hispanic child she identified through an Adoption Exchange listing. The adoption disrupted. While the child demonstrated many behaviors that convinced the adopting parents she did not want to attach, it was also clear that there was a poor match between the new child and the family and shortcutting in the placement process.

The politeness and respect for privacy that characterized this family of English background had matched well the dignity and humor of their Oriental daughters. There was order, loving consideration, and quiet sharing of feelings. Their new child was intrusive, abrasive, and loud. She embarrassed her sisters publicly and violated their sense of "our family" by airing her complaints to any who would listen. There are families in which her style would fit—they are loosely organized, affectionate and outgoing, and generally communicate their feelings at the top of their lungs. This child could probably have settled into such a family. But the English family was violating its essential nature as it tried to accommodate the newcomer, and finally the strain became too much to tolerate. If the worker had known the adopting family and the child better, this disruption would have been prevented because the placement would not have been made in the first place.

External pressure. Some adoptions disrupt because pressure against the adoption from extended family or community prove to be more than the adopting family can deal with. The pain involved in such disruptions and the guilt and anger felt on all sides are enormous. Everything possible should be done to help a family working on an adoption that is being pressured from outside the family. Cross-racial placements deserve special scrutiny before placement, in view of the possible hurt to a child if the community disapproves and disrupts an adoption.

Other Failures

We have written as though only actual disruption can be described as an adoption failure. Of course, that is not true, but other kinds of measures are very hard to access. Some very influential members of the adult-adoptee search movement would probably rate their own adoptions as failures, though they would meet the description Professor Kadushin used for success. In the final analysis, only the participants in a particular adoption can decide whether that experience was on the whole a success or failure for them.

What Can You Do?

If you are thinking as you read that your adoption experience was a failure, do not let your thinking remain at that point. Every experience God brings into our lives is intended for our good and can bring us closer to him. It is time to take this experience of failure a few steps further.

Look at Original Goals

It is possible that you had unrealistic goals or expectations for yourselves. Some people seem to have a tendency to set goals, reach them, and then almost unconsciously raise the goal. This tends to leave them feeling that they have failed to achieve what they set out to do. What was your original goal in taking this child? Did you meet that?

When you set your goal, were you aware to what extent the child was a "given" in a situation that was only subject to your efforts and hard work to a limited degree? Perhaps you set a goal and thought it was all up to you. It never was, of course, and you should not take to yourself failure feelings for circumstances and actions that were not under your control. These include all the history and personality that your child brought to the situation, plus the actions and responses that became intertwined with yours and helped to bring about consequences for both of you.

None of us does the best he can all the time. Sometimes we permit ourselves to stubbornly pursue actions that are contrary to God's purposes or break his laws. Our children can be hurt by these actions. If, from the perspective you have now, you feel rightly guilty over your conduct as a parent toward this child, the usual Christian course is open to you. God requires our repentance, restitution so far as possible, change of behavior in the future, and acceptance of his cleansing and forgiveness. He does not desire us to wallow in guilt, misery, and a sense of failure—and to do so is to continue to sin against his love and mercy.

Disruptive Processes

If you are having serious concerns that the adoption situation in your home is going out of control, what should you do? If you adopted through an agency, contact the agency at once and request a visit promptly by a social worker. This should be considered an emergency and scheduling arranged to begin to deal with the situation promptly. If your own social worker is no longer in the agency or is unavailable, you will need to see another worker. In some cases a new worker may be preferable, since defensiveness about the placement can get in the way of good decisions in the present. Some agencies offer family therapy through their counseling units rather than the adoption unit, but it is best to start with the adoption social worker.

If you adopted independently, locate an adoption agency (see the section in chapter 3 on choosing an agency) and take your problem to that agency at once. There you are more likely to find a person who has dealt with a similar situation before and can help you take the steps necessary or make a good referral rather than if you go to a mental-health clinic or local lawyer, for example.

If the agency and you agree that actual disruption of the adoption is the best solution, the worker will know the proper legal steps in your state and what your further responsibilities will be. The agency will also be in a position to help you arrange for the child's care, either by undertaking a new placement for the child or making other arrangements. You may be tempted to send the child to boarding school or in some other way provide for your legal responsibilities without admitting to anyone that the adoption did not succeed. Some such arrangements may need to be worked out, but you should explore all the possibilities with an experienced adoption worker. It is wrong to deny the child an opportunity to be adopted into another family if there is a reasonable possibility that this could be worked out. Try to remember that regardless of how this child may be acting to undermine the placement, he does need adult help.

Family Recovery

Once the disruption process is complete, your family will need time to recover. At first there will probably be a sense of relief: "It feels so good when it quits hurting." But you have come through a very difficult experience and, after a period of numbness, will probably begin to have feelings of doubt, disappointment, grief, and guilt. There may be anger directed toward the agency for a bad placement, toward your spouse for not being more patient, toward the child for being so ungrateful. The list could go on. Try to be honest with yourself about your feelings. Share them with your spouse and listen to your spouse as well.

Because we are addressing this book to Christians, we want to say something further about guilt. All broken relationships are a reminder of human sinfulness. In varying degrees, all parties to a disruption probably contributed by things done and undone reflecting the tragic effects of sin in the situation. True guilt for the sinful acts and attitudes must be acknowledged and forgiveness sought. In addition, some adults may have lingering guilty feelings because they did not measure up to an ideal they had. After all, when God adopts us he never changes his mind or rejects us because we are difficult or bad! You changed your mind and rejected a child, and it troubles you. But you are not God, and he offers us forgiveness—not cheaply but at the price of the death of his Son—when we fail, as in adoption disruption. You need to claim his forgiveness. Some adults may go over the situation continually, trying to see what they could have done differently and perhaps honestly finding nothing. When this happens it is time again to accept the past as a "given" and go on to new opportunities.

If there are other children in the family, they also need help. They wonder how they will explain this to their friends and what to say when teachers ask questions. They may need reassurance that a good living arrangement has been found for the child. Occasionally some further contact with the former family member is needed. If your other children are adopted, their own security with you may be threatened by this disruption. Be sure to offer reassurance.

As in any injury, there will be scars. They can be healthy reminders of what the family tried to do, why it didn't work out as planned, and what the family received and learned from the experience. Families grow by sharing pain as well as joy. If you plan to adopt again, the whole experience can be valuable as you begin again the process of assessing your family, locating a child, and bringing that child into your family.

Failures on the Way

In the case of both actual disruption and adoptions that have unsatisfactory outcomes that appear less dramatic, there are small failures along the way, difficulties through the months that lead to the final feelings of failure. This section will deal with some of those problems and present some intervention suggestions and ideas that have helped families to get their adoption on track toward success after rocky periods.

Dealing with Attachment Difficulties

As discussed before, in both actual disruption and in emotional evaluation of the success of adoptions, the feeling that parents and child did or did not become attached to one another is very significant. For that reason, a number of researchers and clinical workers have tried to look at parent-child attachment, decide what components there are in the process, and how these can be made available in the experience of the adopting parent and child. They do not guarantee attachment—no techniques can—but will help to structure the situation to enhance the possibilities.

In the newborn infant/mother situation the following factors are present ideally: The mother feels a sense of being entitled to parent this child; she has received validation that she is able to parent the child; she is adequately prepared to handle parenting her baby; various family members gather to welcome the new baby into the larger family; and the baby responds to the mother's attentions. In short, positive interactions take place. There is evidence that the baby is predisposed to attach to a caretaker, and certain physiological changes in the mother also assist in attachment bonding.

With some effort, all of the above (except the physiological changes) can be present in an adoption. However, unless you plan for them, they may be missing, especially in the case of the adoption of an older child. When an adoption is arranged, it is well to include planning of details that facilitate attachment—

otherwise they are less likely to happen because they do not have the automatic social support of newborn-baby customs.

Entitlement. Unless her child is very much unwanted by her, or she is feeling societal disapproval for having the baby, the mother of a newborn who has carried a child through pregnancy feels entitled to that baby. Adopting parents may need encouragement in this area. There may be lingering doubts about their lack of biological children or whether this child is the one they are supposed to have. The message of society that only biological parents are real parents may linger in their minds. Preparation for adoption should include talking about what constitutes entitlement to parenthood, and social workers should be certain that the child is actually legally and morally free for adoption. Entitlement is also given to biological parents through the customs of birth announcements, flowers, gifts, congratulations, and offers of help. To the extent possible, adoptive families and friends should modify and use these customs to help the child and the parents feel they are entitled to belong together. Religious ceremonies mark the entrance of a new baby into the family and into the religious body. Many churches now have special ceremonies to welcome adoptive children, and this may be appropriate in your case.

Validation. The primary way parents have a sense of validation of their parenthood is that the child responds to them in such a manner as to say, "You are a good parent to me." In many, many older-child adoptions this is not going to happen for months or even years. Rather, the child may communicate the opposite. We know that insecure parents of newborns sometimes misread quite normal infant behavior as rejection, and a negative pattern may be established that interferes with bonding. Parents will need to be well prepared for the fact that the child may be unable to give validation of their parenthood. A careful social worker can provide some outside validation and should be certain to do so. Genuine appreciation of the adopting parents' humanitarian motives may help. The social worker might say (outside the child's hearing), "We really appreciate what you are doing for Billy." A good fit between what the parent can provide and what the child obviously needs may give satisfaction, even if the child cannot acknowledge it. Other adults can comment on a healthier look or improved homework preparation. Relatively minor satisfactions should be provided as much as possible while you wait for the development of loving relationships, which are the best validation of parenthood. Spouses should be sure to offer each other verbal encouragement and reassurance, and adoptive-parents groups can also play a valuable role in supporting their members through the new placement period.

Preparation for parenthood. As the nuclear family has become smaller and more isolated, we have gradually become aware that young biological parents do not necessarily have any experience or preparation for parenthood. The lack of preparation may lead to early errors that start a cycle of difficulty, or to insecurity on the part of the parents that interferes with bonding, and may be part of a background for abuse and neglect. Consequently we have begun to pay a good bit of attention to prenatal classes and other methods of educating for parenthood. Obviously, similar parenthood preparation should be available to and used by parents who plan to adopt. The materials should include the standard developmental information about children, plus specific help in recognizing and handling the needs of adopted children, especially older ones.

Emotional intensity. Attachments between human beings seem to be fostered by periods of high emotion. The circumstances surrounding birth provide many such moments. Although adoption circumstances will probably be intense emotionally, sometimes the emotions expressed may be sorrow or anger. But even negative feeling can contribute to emotional closeness. Our family often came closest to a foster child who initially was most angry or fought staying with us. The hours spent holding him close and rocking, or rubbing her back so she could relax and go to sleep, led to feelings of tenderness and warmth for the child and good feelings as we felt the child accept comfort. Some older children resent being touched by strangers but, if possible, you should capitalize on such moments of emotional vulnerability to build closeness.

Pleasant interactions. Attachment also develops out of repeated and mutually satisfactory interactions. These are not extraordinary events but just part of the routines of family living. Mother prepares a good dinner and the child eats heartily. Dad sits through a long, boring Little League game and is rewarded with seeing his new child's first hit. After a period of struggle, the rituals of bedtime become a source of pleasure to both. All of this takes time, and sometimes considerable effort must be used in planning and carrying out small exchanges so that they can be mutually pleasurable.

One study found that three out of four adoptive parents of older children felt that their child belonged to them in a month, but that leaves a large number who need more time. Human relationships develop over time—the important thing is to keep satisfactory interactions going. Neither parent nor child should give in to the tendency to withdraw because some interactions are painful or disappointing. Practice reading, sitting with, hugging, expressing affection and other intimate actions. They will become more pleasurable over time as the child learns how to respond. Sometimes I have given a child directions: ''I like it if, when I hug you, you hug me back'' or ''You are allowed to say what you feel about that and I promise not to yell at you about it.'' Remember that you may be very different from adults your child has known in the past, and he has to *learn* by trial and error what to expect of you and what responses will be safe and pleasant in his new home.

Habitual Character-Pattern Failures

Some adoptive families experience persistent difficulty with their older-child adoptions because—although they feel they have worked very hard and consistently and have been as patient and understanding as they can—their child is still reacting and behaving very much as he did months or years before when he joined the family. Over time the family assesses this child as ''stubborn, rebellious, distant, bad,'' or some other set of names that are essentially a moral judgment on the child. The way the child's behavior is carried out may vary, but any recurring behavior pattern provides evidence that the child has an underlying way of responding to situations, and it is not being modified by what the family does to any measurable degree. At this point the adoptive family is apt to be very discouraged.

Actually, the family has intuitively hit on a problem that is common in older adoptive children. These children have developed habitual ways of coping with life. While the patterns are working, they may go unnoticed. For example, a girl who is passive-aggressive in coping style may be pleasant and agreeable to workers and other children in a group-home setting. Unless someone takes particular notice, it may not become apparent that regardless of what the child *says*, she never actually carries out an action unless it suits her. Another child may have learned to cope by escape—even going so far as to engage in activities that lead the caseworker to move him. Because it is very common for a child to have a series of caseworkers, no one may have noticed that the child has repeatedly triggered the frequent moves on his record. Now, for the first time, the child is in a home with one or two adults to keep track of one or several children on a fairly consistent basis. It becomes very apparent that the girl passively accepts directions but then does as she pleases, and that she agrees pleasantly that she has done so and then does it again. Or the boy may try harder and harder to trigger rejection, which always has been his experience before. In these situations it is frustrating to see the child rigidly maintain his or her pattern, even though it does not fit the present situation.

These children are not easy to help, and we believe you should have competent outside counseling. As long as their systems are working, there is no discomfort to lead them to change their methods, and you may find yourself resentful that *you* are changing in ways you don't like just to accommodate them. Be careful that the counselor you choose does not take the approach that if you can manage to change yourself enough, the child will respond with change in the direction you want. It is more likely that the child will change only if his methods no longer work and he is uncomfortable enough to do the work to change—and has good direction and help given through an experienced counselor.

Remember that these habitual ways of coping were developed out of necessity to deal with situations that were very difficult and unpleasant for the child. You can respect the attempt to manage even as you try to help him adopt a better way of handling his life. It is likely that the style adopted will remain to a considerable degree, but you can settle for behavior within the bounds acceptable in your family. One of the books recommended in the list at the end of the book is *No More Here and There* by Ann Carney. The book and epilogue cover five years in the adoption of their son Joey. Mrs. Carney summarizes this type of problem by saying that from the perspective of Mr. Carney and herself, Joey has changed very little inside, although others frequently comment on the change and improvement in the boy. This is encouraging, for it seems to say that although the basic coping style of a child may still be present and apparent to those close to him, behaviors can be brought into a range that is agreeable to the family and world in which he lives and thus make his life pleasanter and better. It is the work of the Holy Spirit to change the inner man in all of us to conform to Christ, and as we work to change behaviors we must pray as well for inner healing of the child's personality.

Moral Development

We expect that the majority of those reading this book will be Christians who take seriously any failure in moral development. Even though their child is developing well physically and intellectually, they will be concerned if that development is not guided by sound moral development. If there appears to be failure in this area, so that there are signs of lying, cheating, stealing, illicit sexual behavior, profanity, blasphemy, disregard for spiritual or religious duties, or other lack of moral development, the parents will not likely feel their adoption is a success. What can you do?

We do not intend to speak lightly of any of the behaviors listed above or others we could mention, so please do not interpret the following comments as excusing those behaviors. They are intended to help you deal with them.

Compared to the amount of research given to other aspects of development, very little time and money has been spent to learn the effects of childhood deprivation and poor parenting on moral development. But what we do have is clear. Children who have neglectful or abusive parents, or who have parents who set bad moral examples, or who have been moved from place to place and experienced one rejection after another, usually have cumulative retardation in their moral development. A ten-year-old with that type of experience may not have the concepts of rules, right and wrong, or authority, which ordinarily develop in a child by age six. A fourteen-year-old may operate on a hedonistic principle ("I do what makes me feel good"), which ordinarily should be outgrown in moral development during the primary-school years. This cumulative lag is not going to disappear overnight when the child is placed in a good home. Nor will it disappear automatically. Just as educational and physical deficits require specific remedial steps, so do deficits in moral development. Here are some suggestions:

Try to figure out what level the child is actually operating on by comparing his behaviors to other children, or by having his moral development tested, if that is possible. This will help you to respond to the behavior at the level he presently understands—and at the same time move on to a higher level of expectations.

Involve the child as much as possible in decision making and hold him responsible for those decisions. These may have to be relatively unimportant decisions at first, but you must begin somewhere. Very likely he has not been held accountable, and even punishments have seemed to come from outside with no connection to his behaviors. For example, in a little girl's memories, one time she was spanked for taking a cookie without permission, but another time it was ignored. She assumes that spanking is associated with her mother's mood, not with her taking a cookie.

Be warmly affectionate with the child. Parents who are perceived by their children as aloof or distant make it difficult for the child to identify with them. Identification with a morally responsible adult is one way a child learns moral behavior.

Help the child learn moral behaviors. There are many books on the market to help you in this area. If you need some background, visit the church library and read what is available, beginning with the youngest ages, or contact a Christian agency or counseling center for suggestions. You will find a multitude of suggestions for handling specific problems and for teaching particular virtues like sharing or respect for group decisions or property. Remember to begin your teaching according to the child's moral-development age, but don't talk down to him or make him feel silly. Adapt the suggestions to his physical and mental age. For example, begin to teach a young child the joy of sharing by letting him pass around cookies. It would be more appropriate to help an older child earn some money for the Salvation Army's Christmas kettle or a charity of *his* choice. But what do you do if he earns the money, then decides he wants a new sweater instead? If you think about it, that sounds very like the three-year-old who decides to eat all the cookies. You would not permit the one, and you should not permit the other. Hold him to his commitment, even if he is no longer a cheerful giver. He is just learning how to give—cheerfulness will have to wait.

Christian morality accompanies the new birth. In some persons it precedes, and in all it follows. You cannot force your child to become a Christian. You can help the child develop moral standards and behaviors and you can pray for conversion, which will give inner meaning and direction to outwardly moral behavior.

School Failure

Some adoptions that are moving along quite well inside the family can come under great stress because the child is failing in school. Academic difficulties and/or behavior problems will get the child in trouble at school and spill over into the rest of his life. There are books available with good ideas about helping the family do schoolwork together to help the child succeed, and we will not take space to give that information here. But we do want to add some special material with respect to adopted children, especially those who have had repeated separations before they came to live in their permanent family.

Dr. Nir Littner of Chicago, Illinois, has studied the effect on school behavior of separations in the past. His work will be helpful to you. Dr. Littner points out that there are many small separations in the life at school, and to react to them is natural. This can happen at graduation, when some anxiety and sense of loss is reasonable. It could involve changing schools, which almost all children find somewhat threatening. Or it could be the separation from teacher involved in a school vacation or the Friday-to-Monday break, although exaggerated distress over this separation would be unusual. Some children are also more vulnerable to feeling anxious over separations, and adopted children may fit in this category. Vulnerability is affected by earlier separations and the degree and kind of resolution of those separations. There is the strength of a psychological trigger—death of a beloved teacher may link up in the child's mind with the death of his mother. And there is the matter of total stress in the child's life—which may be very high in early stages of placement, a birthday, or other special times.

Schoolchildren who are feeling separation anxiety may show this in learning problems, undesirable behavior patterns, or such things as school phobia. Learning problems develop for several reasons. In order for learning to take place, there needs to be a carrier wave between the student and teacher. If the child has been repeatedly separated from adults in the past, he may not have "object constancy,"—or the perception that the teacher is involved with him when absent. For such a child, learning only takes place when the teacher is there and in touch with him. The student may also have trouble learning from more than one teacher. Or he may have trouble learning because his mental processes are so taken up in dealing with separation. This tends to occur at particular times, as when a substitute replaces the regular teacher, when holidays are approaching, or at the end of the year when leaving the teacher is imminent.

Your child may show his anxiety in school behavior problems. One of the most common for children who have been repeatedly rejected in the past is to use behavior that says clearly, "I'll reject you first." There may be truancy, running away, or dropping out—escape routes we mentioned in connection with character traits. Some children use a technique that says, "I'll withhold, and you'll holler about that work, and I'll know you are still interested in me." Other children act as though they are using sour-grapes defenses: "You are no good and have nothing I want, so I won't have to worry about losing you."

Of course, just because you can understand why a child is failing in school does not mean you can accept it. If you decide that part of the problem may be difficulty with separations, you can minimize additional separations while trying to resolve old difficulties in this area and build confidence in the permanence of present relationships. Choose carefully the school and the classroom for your child, with his anxieties and limitations in mind. Develop a good relationship with the teacher and discuss Dr. Littner's material as you jointly work on the problem. There is a citation in the bibliography.

Try to avoid letting school failure spill over and spoil all the areas where your child *is* succeeding. Provide chances for success in other areas and give general encouragement and specific help. A child is not a failure nor is an adoption a failure because the child is not doing well in school.

Getting Help

In several sections of this chapter we have suggested that you may need outside help to get the adoption back on track and moving ahead again. But whom should you ask for help? If you adopted through an agency, talk to its personnel first. They need to be aware of problems in the adoption before crisis points are reached and can often provide the experienced counseling you need. If they cannot help you or refer you elsewhere for help, look for resources within your church or school. If you are persistent, you can find available help within your family budget.

Do not park your parental judgment outside the door when you step into the counselor's office. Do not be defensive or hostile, but do participate actively in the counseling process. If the relationship does not develop into a joint effort by all of you to solve the problem, find a new source of help. As in every occupation, there are competent and incompetent people and varying approaches. The comments made previously about finding an agency with

which you are philosophically compatible are in order again as
you look for advice and counsel from professionals.

Failure Traps for Christians

Failure does not discriminate on the basis of creed, race,
marital state, or sex. But there are some traps on the path to
failure in adoption that seem particularly set for Christians. Let us
turn to them now—and to ways to avoid them.

"Everything Is Perfect" Syndrome

Some well-meaning Bible teachers and preachers have had so
much to say about praising God in all our circumstances and living
victoriously that a portion of today's Christians believes it is a sin
to fail or to have feelings of failure. Consequently, they deny to
themselves that they are having difficulties and present a smiling
face to anyone who asks about their lives. They may maintain this
front until everything falls in around them and then feel quite
bitter and angry toward God and others because they relied on a
false understanding of God's promises. A few minutes spent
thinking over God's dealings with some of his closest disciples
reveals that they experienced disappointments, failures, set-
backs, and difficulties. David and Saul, Jeremiah and Peter,
Miriam and Mary—the Bible reveals not just their triumphs and
emotional highs, but their failures and periods of discouragement. And, in each case, God responded to their situation with
healing and encouragement as it was needed.

Adoption is not all smooth sailing—neither is biological parenthood. We set ourselves up for failure when we pretend that all is
well and cut ourselves off from help from God and others when all
is not well.

"I'm in a Hurry"

Being a parent is a lifetime commitment, and the dividends of
our investment in a child may be a very long time coming. Some
parents do not live long enough to know that their child has
entered the kingdom. Other parents never achieve a truly close

and loving relationship with their child. But a sure path to failure is trying to hurry things along. We must give adoptive relationships time to develop. We must work and pray and wait. God adopts us. Then he begins to change us so we look like members of his family. We must learn to be patient, as he is patient.

Overindulgence in "Things"

None of us would profess to believe that we can buy love. All of us talk about the hazards of materialism. But some adoptive parents nevertheless set themselves a failure trap by giving their children too much. We don't set out to do this, but it happens—and there are many reasons why. When we accept into our home a child whose background is poverty and deprivation, we tend to want to make up for the lost years for the child. Or we have waited many years for a child to dress, to buy toys for, to inhabit a dream bedroom—so we make up for lost time for ourselves. Or if the child has learned to manipulate people to get material things to replace the love he no longer hopes to have, we fall in with the game, hoping he will interpret our gifts as love. Biological parents overindulge their children, too, but adoptive parents have all the reasons they have, plus some extras. We must discipline ourselves to avoid giving too much, too soon, or too easily in material things.

Insecurity in Discipline

Some adoptive parents feel insecure about disciplining their child and consequently may over- or under-discipline, or discipline in an erratic way. This may grow out of an attitude that says, "I have waited so long for this beautiful gift from God. How can I hurt the child by denying this thing he wants or by punishing this behavior?" Another parent may feel insecure about his or her right to be the child's real parent. Especially in discipline situations, the child may openly challenge the parent with "You aren't my real mother [or father]." God has given you this child to parent—you are entitled to exercise discipline over him. You may wish to re-read the previous section on feeling entitled to parenthood.

Blaming the Genes

Biological parents who see a behavior they don't like in a child may say in a half-kidding way, "He must have gotten that from *your* side of the family." Adoptive parents can take the blaming one step further: "He must have gotten that from his biological family." Certainly, inherited tendencies and abilities play a part in behavior, as do the experiences your child had before coming to your family. But all of us could go clear back to Adam blaming someone else for our difficulties and shortcomings. When we are tempted to blame a current situation on the genes, we should check ourselves. Instead of asking, "Who or what can we blame for this?" we should ask, "What do we need to do about this?" This brings the difficulty into the realm of the present, where something can be done to solve the problem. Finding a scapegoat solves nothing, and it can become a habitual way of avoiding dealing with problems in the adoptive family.

The "Chosen Child" Syndrome

At one time adoption literature was full of the phrase "chosen child," and adopting parents were advised to emphasize that their relationship with the child was a matter of choice and somehow superior to the supposedly involuntary relationship of biological parents and children. Aside from the fact that this seems to belittle the providence of God in all relationships, it has other problems. If you emphasize too heavily that you chose this child, you increase his feeling of risk that you might change your mind. After all, he may already be dealing with the fact that his birth mother did not choose to keep him. If you have both biological and adopted children in your family, it may lead to barriers between them that are unnecessary and hurtful. The idea of "choosing" itself may be more fiction than reality in today's adoption system. After all, what were your actual choices? Did you take this child because it was your choice, or because God led you into a situation where you believe it was his will for you to parent this child? Some adult adoptees have told us that the thought of being chosen was very precious to them. Today, when we no longer have more babies than families to adopt them, the ring of truth could be missing from the adoption story if we insist on emphasizing the chosen-child theme.

The adoption process is one with the possibility for much joy but also with the potential for failure. These failures can be large, as when the adoption is rejected and then legally negated. Or they can be small, such as when you feel inadequate for not handling a situation as you wish you had. In all the trials and failures you need the supportive concern of friends, fellow Christians, and members of your family. Childrearing is never without difficulty and at times we must each turn the situation over to the Lord. Our parental responsibility is to be faithful to the task of rearing a child. God's responsibility is to fulfill his promises of help in time of need. With his supporting love the burden of childrearing is lightened, and the yoke is made bearable in the midst of failures, big and small.

9

When the Child Grows Up

Many people who want to adopt a child have doubts and fears, not necessarily concerning their ability to parent a child, but about handling adoption questions with the child. Parents' concerns generally center around two issues:

What shall we say when our adopted child asks specific questions, and what effects will our answers have?

Will our adopted child want to search for birth parents?

First we will try to give you some information about answering questions in general. Naturally we won't try to provide detailed questions and specific replies, since in our experience children don't ask the questions we're exactly prepared for anyway! They don't ask them at the right times either. But we will provide typical themes of adoptee concerns and some general principles for making your answers.

In the second section we will add some ideas about the so-called "search," a shorthand way of speaking about all the issues involved in coming to terms with adoption as the child matures into an adult. Typically these include handling of records, contacts between children and birth parents, planned and unplanned intrusions from the past, and considerations for changing the adoption system toward more openness. Some adult adoptees and birth parents have been willing to discuss their own adoption experience and tell us what questions were important and why, and what they want in connection with their search for information and identity.

Questions and Answers

Before you try to answer questions for your child, perhaps you need to answer some for yourself.

Your Own Questions

Many Christians have unconsciously absorbed the idea that one man joined to one woman for life, plus an indefinite number of children, constitutes God's ideal family. Families that do not fit that mold are often seen as "second best" and are viewed as God's accommodation to human failure. It will help you answer your child's doubts and fears if by faith you believe in God's overruling love and providence for your special kind of family. He didn't second-guess himself. He *planned* this for you and for your adopted child.

You will also need faith to believe that this child is exactly as he was meant to be. Surely there are secondary causes and human responsibility, but the child as he comes to you—disabled or physically perfect, intelligent or mentally slow, a brand-new baby or an emotionally scarred ten-year-old—is exactly as God meant him to be at this point and is intended as a blessing to the child and others. Believing this requires you to trust the wisdom and love of God to cover and redeem the past.

Adoption also asks you to live in the present by faith. This child is where he is meant to be *now*. He may leave you, search out his original family, and rejoin them. Did you ever wonder how Pharaoh's daughter felt when Moses eventually chose his own people? You cannot worry about the *what if's* of the future. Answer today's questions the best you can. As God enables you, do the best job of parenting and enjoying the present. It is the very best preparation for the future. The strengths, skills, and love built into your adopted child now will always be there for him to draw on. If you think that asks too much, remember that all parents must eventually let their children go, and many lose children to death before adulthood. By faith, all of us can leave the future of our children in God's hands.

By faith, you can believe that you have been specially prepared by God to parent this particular child now. God has used circumstances and gifts in your life so that you are adequately prepared. However, you will not always feel that way, and questions and confrontations around adoption may especially threaten your sense of competence to parent the child.

When Evelyn was a young mother struggling through a difficult period with an adopted child, an older Christian woman advised her to memorize and meditate on 2 Timothy 1:7 until it became a part of her childrearing: "For God hath not given us the spirit of fear; but of power, and of love, and of a sound mind."

God gave you power (authority) to parent this child. This child is in your charge by the will of God and you are accountable to God.

God gave you love for this child. When you feel angry, hurt, or revengeful because of things said or done, remember that God is the source of all love and will enable you to love this child as required.

God is the source of a sound mind. He will give you the wisdom to use your authority and love to handle the situation that is before you at a particular time. You do not need to feel flustered, fearful, or defensive as you meet adoption questions and controversies. Relax, recall the promises of this verse, and answer the need of the present from the reserves of your confidence in God.

Ask God to use the Scriptures and all the means by which he brings his grace into your lives to build up your faith in his plans for you and your child. This is the first step in transmitting faith to your child and preparing you for the child's questions.

Some General Principles

Using Bible knowledge. It is helpful to build into your family's general Bible knowledge the background for future questions. Be sure Bible stories are known to the child that may help all of you see your situation in the framework of God's variety of plans for families. It will be better if this information comes into the child's understanding naturally, not in a time of crisis or questioning when introduction of Bible stories may seem artificial or forced. What are such stories? Mephibosheth, the disabled son of Jonathan who came to live with David after his beloved father's death; Hannah, who prayed for and was given children; Pharaoh's daughter who instantly loved and wanted to care for a stranger's child; Moses' parents, who gave him up so he could be protected and educated; Timothy, whose parents reflected different ethnic and religious backgrounds; John the Baptist, the only child of middle-aged parents; Daniel and his friends, who went to live in a "boarding school"; and many more. These nontypical situations reflect God's diversity of plans for families.

Watch your language. This is a good time to mention another aspect of adoption—the words we use to talk about it. Many parents have difficulty knowing how to describe various people and transactions in the adoption situation. In writing this chapter and throughout the book, we have tried to use a vocabulary for adoption as summarized and explained by Marietta Spencer. She deals with such usages as "my own son" and "my adopted son," when it is correct and when not to say, "first mother," the right words to use with your child in describing adoption, and so forth. Information about her article is in the bibliography, and you will find it very helpful. The words we use to talk about adoption help keep our thinking clear and avoid unnecessary confusion or hurt to ourselves or others. It is worth the effort to learn to use an accurate, positive adoption vocabulary.

Your Child's Questions

With these preparation ideas in mind, let us move to some specific questions your adopted child may ask. The most basic question is asked in a hundred different ways but is essentially

"Why was I adopted?" Your child will understand as he grows that most children live with one or both parents throughout childhood. He will have friends whose parents die, whose parents divorce, whose parents are not married, whose parents are very poor, whose parents fight a great deal. All the reasons he can think of, or which may have been told to him by adults at some point, will not necessarily explain his own situation to him satisfactorily. Because of general attitudes in books they read, movies they see, talk shows they watch, even casual conversations they hear, adopted children will form some idea that adoption is an unusual situation. Probably your child will ask questions to try to figure out why he is part of an adoption. For some people, adoption is not regarded positively. Especially in some groups, parents who permit their children to be adopted are censured or regarded as less loving of their babies. Pregnant girls find that their peers urge them to abort rather than permit adoption, or to accept welfare and keep the baby, and they frequently question their motives in allowing adoption. Some adults express the idea that people who have babies should have to rear them, as though rearing babies is a punishment for sinful behavior. In carefully designed research, reported recently in *Child Welfare*, investigators found that the adoption option was not mentioned to *most* unmarried girls requesting pregnancy services. I have been in hospital maternity units where nurses were openly hostile toward young mothers planning to surrender their babies for adoption. Even if your child avoids the trap of learning to think that his birth parents were bad people who used adoption to dispose of something they didn't want, he may decide instead that he was a troublesome, unlovable child whom good, normal people would not want to have. This may have been unintentionally reinforced by hearing such comments as "You're so lucky to have parents like the Smiths" or, after ordinary misbehavior, "You should be ashamed to treat your parents like that when they were kind enough to adopt you." Such remarks are not infrequent and often come from people who should know better.

Encouragingly, many children weather all this very well, accept their adoptive parents' love, and identify with their new families.

They shrug off their doubts, latch on to an explanation that suits them, and stick with it. Others are not so lucky. They mull silently over their dilemma and may ask questions in different disguises. One adoptive parent was puzzled about a rash of stories and questions about illegitimate teenage parents and what happened to their babies. Their daughter was actually the child of divorced parents, so no connection was apparent between her birth situation and these stories. But it developed that she had secretly pieced together bits of accurate and inaccurate information and decided that her mother and father had been forced to marry by an unwanted pregnancy—herself. It was tremendously helpful to this girl to learn that she had come into the world inside a marriage originating in love, even though it ended in divorce.

Unanswerable questions. If every explanation may be in the end unsatisfactory, you need to know how to answer "Why was I adopted?" or such variants as "Why did my mother go away?" or "How come I had to live with you?" Here are some general guidelines:

1. *Tell the truth*. Any explanation you give should be honest. Some parents are tempted to make the story less than true because they wish to spare the child hurt or do not want to seem unfair to people they did not know. If you have honestly faced the truth in your own mind and forgiven and accepted the child's parents, your child will sense that he can do the same, even if pain is involved.

2. *Don't give the child more than he can handle*. Truth or not, there are some facts a child should not be forced to consider until he is more mature. Use truthful generalities that fit the situation, but do not harrow the child's imagination. Since some children will be perfectly satisfied with rather small amounts of information— don't pile on more than is needed. Try to answer in the same commonsensical way you try to satisfy a question like "Why doesn't Jamie like me?" or "What happens to the sun at night?" You should judge the child's understanding, give suitable information you can build on later, and give it in a way that increases the child's trust in himself and others.

3. *Don't postpone to avoid answering*. Whenever possible, the child

should have an answer at the time he asks. If you are busy, if there are people around with whom you don't want to share information, if you need to look up some information, or if you need to think about your answer, say so. But you must take the initiative to come back to the question rather than hope the child will forget about it.

Information questions. Another group of questions is summarized as "What were my parents like?" This question arises in many different situations but tends to be associated with attempts to understand oneself and plan for the future. An adopted daughter with a continual weight problem wanted to know, "Was my mother fat?" Now living in a skinny family, she wondered whether heredity could explain her difference. Another teenager wanted to be tall and was assessing his chances by trying to learn the height of his birth parents. Sometimes the questions reflect nothing more than curiosity. Don't you wonder sometimes about relatives who were dead before you were born or cousins you haven't seen? If you know little about the parents, you will have to say so. Don't make up descriptions. But do not imply that the questions are improper or unreasonable. For example, you can say —to a child who asks, "What color was my mother's hair?"—"I don't know that. Nobody ever told us." Follow with some positive comment about her such as, "Anyway, aren't we glad you wound up with such pretty brown hair." Perhaps you could add, "You know, I'm shorter than both Grandpa and Grandma. I wonder sometimes who gave me that shortness." Or you might say, "This seems to be important to you. Since I don't know, let's contact the agency and ask if we can get an answer."

Some "What were my parents like?" questions have a moral tone. Moral development touches all areas of a child's life. Many young adolescents become very good-versus-bad in their thinking. They may reassess their adoption and attempt to decide the morality of their parents' actions. Now the question becomes "Who was to blame?" It is little use to try to convince a child this age that the question doesn't have any answer we have the right to give. Once again, be honest but not cruel or *unnecessarily* explicit. Give all sides, although the adolescent may express some strong negative opinions. For example, a group of 14-year-old girls uniformly expressed strong disapproval of a girl their age who placed her child for adoption, even when the social workers attempted to give good reasons why she chose that plan. Don't argue. Young people usually become more reasonable and fair as they mature and are able to temper moral judgments with compassion. There may be a temptation to silently agree with your child, an agreement your child will probably sense. There are good reasons not to do this. You need to model Christian forgiveness and acceptance. Practically speaking, the child may outgrow temporary harsh judgments and come to resent the fact that you did not help him do this. If the child adopts a view of his birth parents that implies that *you* were to blame for their "losing" their child, try to avoid these arguments also. Of course it hurts, but the attitude is probably only a temporary conclusion. You can say, "I wish you didn't feel that way, but I can see it looks like that to you. Your dad and I did what we thought right and so did everyone else, and it doesn't help to second-guess now." Avoid identifying your opinions as the will of God. All of us have made mistakes, and our confidence lies in knowing that God brings good out of all. We can restate that confidence without self-justification or sermonizing, both of which may be resented.

Your child will probably have some questions that fit under the heading "How did this happen?" He is looking primarily for facts. As your child develops a sense of time and chronology, he will naturally want to know details about the principal events in his own life: "Where was I born? How much did I weigh? How old was I when you got me? What do they do when you get adopted? Did I go to court, too?" These questions may be very emotionally laden for you but not necessarily so for the child. "Where was I born?" may not mean the child is thinking about adoption at all. It is just he is interested in knowing. Tell him and add: "Let's go by the hospital," if that is possible. The child's friends may be curious about the mechanics of adoption, and he may want to be able to answer them better. People often ask adopted children more personal questions than they do others. Or the trigger may be a routine school assignment. Some questions you can answer, and some require facts you don't have. But, again, get the answers if possible. They will stimulate further discussion.

The more times you have to answer "I don't know" to a question readily answered for most children, the more attention and mystery there will be surrounding adoption. Try to be prepared with the kind of matter-of-fact information your child is likely to want, by getting it when you are going through the adoption process. History gathering was mentioned in chapter 4 as part of the agency's role. Adult adoptees tell us that parents should answer fact questions without making it "a big deal."

Your child will probably also ask questions regarding relatives and about finding his birth family. We are going to cover this kind of question in the next section.

Search

During the last decade, Search has received a great deal of attention in adoption literature, in popular media, and even in legislatures and courtrooms. *Child Welfare*, the leading periodical devoted to social-welfare concerns for children, published approximately sixty articles on adoption between 1973 and 1984. Of these, ten dealt with Search issues. Only articles on special-needs children and cross-cultural adoptions exceeded this number. Agencies are trying to document, understand, and adapt to great change in this area. It is not unusual for a talk-show host to preside over a first meeting between a birth mother and her adopted child, and numerous popular dramas have been built around Search plots. Legislatures and courts in at least eighteen states have modified their statutes regarding confidentiality of adoption records, and other states are considering changes.

There is a great deal of confusion because so many different perspectives must be considered—perspectives of the agency, the adoptee (both as an adult and as a child), birth parents, and adopting families. Lawyers, doctors, journalists, and the-man-in-the-street each see the issues differently. It will help to try to see Search issues from the point of view of all the people involved.

You are likely to look at the questions in a way relevant to where you are in the adoption picture right now. Adults who are already part of an adoption may see Search questions as raising the possibility of major directional changes in midstream: "But I promised that mother to keep her secret." Or "I agreed to take her if her mother never interfered." Other readers are considering adoption but are free to find and agree to any arrangement that seems wise to them now. They want to know what works best. Considering Search issues requires us to think about what they mean to both past and future participants in the adoption process. This applies to those who participate as adoptees, adoptive parents, birth parents, or adoption workers.

How We Got Here

It is helpful to begin consideration of Search issues with some adoption history and summary of some changes that have occurred. The purposes of adoption historically were four: to provide legal heirs, to provide permanent substitute parents, to give children to families, and to provide an option for biological parents unwilling or unable to rear their children. Today, at least in the United States, the paramount reason for adoption is to provide permanent substitute parents for children. We need to recognize that the need for parents does not disappear when the child has been reared to emancipation age. Parents fill a lifelong role in their children's lives. In order to fulfill these purposes, legal protections were granted to all parties. The intent was to create a new family for the child that was identical in all legal respects to a biological family. This new family often waited in considerable anxiety until this final legal step was taken. Adopting parents then felt they would be free of intrusions by outsiders or birth parents. It is worth noting that some older adopted children and some birth parents also felt a sense of relief and security when legal severance and reestablishment of parental roles was complete.

But all was not serene or complete in the case of a significant number of adoptees. Mental health workers first suspected, then documented, that a disproportionate number of adopted children were appearing in their caseloads. Upon reflection, it was realized that this could be for many reasons: adoptive families are more accustomed to seeking help from agencies; teacher and others may *expect* more difficulty from adoptive children and thus refer more quickly; and so on. But the initial statistics fueled concern about adoption. Adult adoptees began to write books that detailed their misery and confusion as they searched for an identity within a shroud of secrecy. Birth mothers, now less afraid of public censure, began to speak of children born and adopted twenty years before, admitting to long-denied feelings of loss and guilt. Although still a minority of all adoption participants, some of these people banded together in organizations and began to press for legislative and judicial rulings that would permit them to see records of their adoption proceedings. Their efforts have often been successful. Where possible, they have enlisted the help of agencies, courts, and legislatures. In addition, they have formed self-help organizations to pool their information and resources. We can expect this movement to continue.

Changes in Society

As we consider how to react to adoption's changing purpose, legal standing, and especially unsealed records, it helps to realize that society today is also different from when the forms of adoption we know best were developed. Our culture is much less inclined to pressure an unwed mother to keep her pregnancy a secret. People in general seem to care less about chastity and related matters of morality. That reaction is unfortunate, but a parallel recognition by Christian churches that forgiveness and restoration should be held out to these women is encouraging. Christian adoption agencies make an effort to help women with problem pregnancies work out the best arrangement for rearing their babies, and absolute secrecy about their situation is usually neither necessary nor wise. Recognizing that his parentage will not stigmatize a child, adopting couples also have less need or desire to hide the circumstances of the child's birth.

The children being adopted are also different. While babies are still being placed, many of the children awaiting adoption are older, and those already in homes were no longer infants when they joined their adopting families. Many were disabled or victims of abuse or neglect and had bounced in and out of various homes and institutions. The typical child in today's adoption may be aware of a great deal about his own past, though often the facts are mixed up and distorted. In the case of younger children, adoption may represent a solution to a very traumatic situation unknown to the child. Many children being currently adopted will not find a pretty story at the end of their search a decade or two from now. Agencies try to clarify and clear up these distortions before adoption, but for various reasons the child may cling to his own version of his life history throughout childhood.

Of course, this has always been true for some adoptees, and today's young women voluntarily placing babies are much like the mothers of previous generations. But involuntary termination of parental rights and court-instigated adoptions are last-resort options in many jurisdictions. Such parents do not lose their children unless they are extremely incompetent as parents and have not been able to change, even with intensive help. These are the parents some adult adoptees will find at the end of the Search.

Values in society have also been reordered. At one time our culture placed a very high priority on privacy. Now intrusions are so frequent that we often take them for granted in situations where our fathers and mothers would have made clear that "That is really not your business." Openness has received a priority that permits family secrets to be aired in dismaying detail. Generally the other members of families involved are not consulted before the divulging member goes public. As we consider Search issues, we need to think carefully about the value of privacy in the development of a sense of security and identity. In addition, theologians once considered that sins done openly and advertised blatantly were more offensive to God. Churches taught that confession to God is essential to the soul, but telling others might cause unnecessary harm. Insisting on total openness about adoption may be one of those situations where one person's unburdening puts an unfair burden on another. On the other hand, improper secrecy may lead to gossip, speculation, or worry that is totally without foundations. As we consider changes in the adoption processes in response to all these other changes, we must find ways to protect what was good in the old system and modify it in ways to improve current adoption practices.

Different Perspectives

Let us now attempt to look at Search issues from the perspectives of the agency or other third parties arranging adoption, the adoptees, the birth families, and the adopting families. In each case we will try to outline some of the concerns and problems, as well as the possibilities for change in each of these elements of the adoption picture.

The agency perspective. Fundamental for the agency is the realization that it has always existed to serve at least three parties—birth parent, adopting parent, and adoptee. There was always the possibility of conflicts of interests and rights between these parties, but it was clear that first priority would be given to the best interests of the child. While in practice the ideal might not have been attained, the intent to make all decisions in the best interest of the child served to clarify much adoption protocol. Most agencies did not expect to continue to serve the child for more than a few months beyond the adoption date. After a brief post-adoption time, the adoption was closed and the agency's service to the child ended.

Now a new class of persons is coming to the agencies. These are adult adoptees asking for help and information. Since the very reason for the existence of social agencies is to help those in need, they must find ways to respond to these people. But they cannot respond in the same ways they did earlier. The adult adoptee is no longer a child whose best interests must be served first. Now three or more *adults* may have conflicting needs, rights, and desires. It is difficult to balance these factors and serve all three parties well. But the agencies cannot in good conscience turn away people in need, nor can they pretend that only a troublemaking and disruptive minority, which needs protection from itself, is asking for birth information. Though only a minority of adult adoptees are involved, they tend to be very pressing, verbal, and insistent that they will not go away. They must be treated with respect.

A major concern from the perspective of the agency is confidentiality. Promises were made, which the agency is obligated to fulfill. These promises were not lightly or capriciously given. Confidentiality had several purposes. First, it was generally believed twenty years ago that security and feelings of permanence were necessary to permit the development of the child's self-image. Social workers knew that even foster children who lived for long periods in one home often had difficulty forming an identity and guessed that it was continued contact with birth families that prevented them from feeling secure. Not wishing to make the same mistakes for adoptees, agency practice included (by means of confidentiality to all parties) cutting off the possibility of intrusions from the past. When possible, some adopting families hid the whole process from others and also from the children themselves, although good agencies did not intend or recommend this practice. We know from adult adoptees that all the secrecy sometimes contributed to their anxiety and interfered with identification with the new family and a sense of belonging.

Confidentiality was also intended to provide privacy. The general public has often had a prying curiosity about adoption. By sealing court records and issuing new birth certificates, the courts and agencies intended to protect the privacy of all concerned parties. Not every Tom, Dick, and Mary would be able to have information. The affected parties were entitled to share it only with those they chose.

Confidentiality also permitted birth parents to begin again. With the knowledge that they had provided a permanent home for their child and the chapter was closed, birth parents were free to make a new start. They relinquished some rights, but they also gained the assurance that the past was behind. This was especially necessary for young unmarried women in the social climate of the day. Many of these women received good help, reordered their lives, and achieved a measure of happiness and success that would not have been possible at the time without confidential adoptions. In summary, having in good faith given and received assurances of confidentiality, the agencies are perplexed as to how to handle requests years later to violate those promises.

Agencies are also aware that adoption is a process that evolved over a long period of time through much trial and error. Requests to open files will have ramifications all through the adoption system, and agencies are concerned with all these effects. Knowing that it is not necessarily a final resolution of the relationship, will needy parents be more reluctant to place their child for adoption? A young father recently told a caseworker, "I want her to have an abortion. I don't want any surprises eighteen years from now." Will the supply of potential adopting parents likewise dwindle? Certainly many adopting families are willing to consider varieties of open adoption, but others are looking for a child to become unquestionably a permanent member of their family for life. Will this possibility be undermined? Will opening records expose the agencies to legal suits for violation of privacy or subject their judgments to the hindsight of people who were not there when a decision had to be made? Will they be placed in a position of trying to prove or defend statements about people placed in records by workers long gone from the agencies? Will society itself view adoption in a less positive way—as a sort of second-best choice, a halfway house for children? Agencies want their perspectives considered in the process of changes under-way, because they, too, have a stake in the process—for themselves and on behalf of the people they served in the past and those they hope to serve in the future.

The adoptees' perspective. Adoptees bring another set of perspectives to the Search issues. Naturally, part of an adult adoptee's perspective is a product of his childhood views and firsthand experiences of adoption. While some of these ideas are distorted, they cannot be ignored. What are these recollections and perceptions, and do they differ for those who search and those who do not?

Why do they search for their origins? Each individual adoptee who sets out to find out more about birth parents has a unique experience and goal, but researchers have attempted to answer this question in various studies, beginning in 1954. They tried to get this information by asking questions of adult adoptees. The earlier studies tended to concentrate only on adult adoptees who were searching for or had found their birth parents. They tended to conclude that these searchers had had either no disclosure of background information to them or only hostile data; that they had had unsatisfactory relationships with their adoptive families; and that they tended to have a negative self-image. In 1975 a carefully designed study found the conclusions about poor relationships with adoptive families not substantiated. Another study in 1979 in England looked at the same questions. They studied the first 500 adult adoptees who took advantage of a change in the law to look at their records. These represented about 1 to 2 percent of those affected by the law. Three-fifths of these said they were looking in order to establish their true self-identities. The majority were stable, well-adjusted individuals who felt they had a right to know their biological origins. Few had been told in a helpful way about their adoption. Some had been told inadequately, some not at all. About 20 percent had problems in their adoptive situation. These findings agree with other studies examining the relationship between self-concept and adoption, where it has been concluded that adoption itself does not produce a negative self-image.

Most studies of adult adoptees have focused on the searchers. Now we are beginning to see studies that compare searchers with non-searchers. In general these studies show that non-searchers have a more positive self-concept, more positive feelings toward adoptive parents, and more positive feelings surrounding their original knowledge that they were adopted. They also had less concern about background in general and knew less about that background. The non-searchers tended to express more happiness with their lives, but 51 percent of the sample of *searchers* said that they were happy or mostly happy.

Beyond the research answers—which are greatly affected by when, how, and what is asked, and who is asking—what reasons do individuals give? A surprising number include a statement like: "I just wanted to see someone who looked like me." Others expressed a need to know "who I am." Others have a sense that their birth parents must also have questions, and they want to show their birth parents that everything turned out okay for them.

Often some kind of life crisis seems to lead to a search for more information. Doctors may ask questions during pregnancy or illness that adoptees find themselves unable to answer. One adoptee never thought much about his biological heritage until he stood looking down at his baby grandson. Quite suddenly he felt an urge to know more about the biological background he had passed on to this descendant. Occasionally the death of adoptive parents sets an adoptee free to conduct a search half-consciously postponed for fear of hurting much-loved people.

Why do adult adoptees think we should say yes to their request to open up the records? Because it confirms to them that they are at least as important in the adoption triangle as the other members. Decisions have been made in their behalf, and they appreciate the goodwill and necessity behind those decisions. But now they wish to be full participants in their own life story. Searchers usually believe as well that they have a legal right to facts concerning their own birth. Many also believe that the knowledge that at some future time records will be open will encourage adoptive families to avoid unnecessary secrecy during the child's growing years, thus fostering trust and honesty between members of adoptive families, agencies, and birth families.

No adult adoptee in a large searcher/non-searcher study felt that sealed records should be open to minors. But what *do* they want us to tell adopted children? There is no one answer, but again some themes surface: "Tell them both good and bad facts, but don't pick on their families. It's like you're picking on them." "Let them know if they have brothers or sisters and what happened to them. Tell them things in ordinary ways—don't make it a big deal." "If he asks if he can find them, tell him the truth and whether you can and will help and when this will happen" [there is a consensus that about twenty is a good age to suggest]."

Some adoptive parents tell us that a child has never asked any questions about the birth family. Counselors tend to discount this, saying that *all* children they see wanted to and tried to ask questions. We're not so sure. The counselors, almost by definition, see only troubled children. In one family we know there are two daughters adopted under similar circumstances from the same agency with the same social worker. One has always asked and received answers to many questions about her adoption. The other daughter asks almost none and seems to find such discussions uninteresting. Both are now teenagers, and it seems unlikely that the parents are suppressing questions from one and not the other. More likely, adopted children differ in their need to search just as adult adoptees do.

It is important to realize that the negative reasons given in early studies do not consistently explain why some adult adoptees do and some do not feel a need for more information or for actual contact with birth families. Perhaps we need to look for explanations in some combination of personality and circumstances. I have a friend who spends her vacations in musty courthouse basements, tracing records of her family tree. Spare money goes to buy research materials, and long, complicated letters are sent and received as she tracks down obscure references to long-dead people. My friend pursues her search with zeal and pleasure, but there is no suggestion of neurotic need or unhappiness with her life. She just likes her hobby. For my part the lifelong labors of a great-aunt would provide a wealth of information and shortcut many difficult trails should I decide to pursue a similar hobby. But I have only a faint interest in such subjects, barely enough to complete the family trees in my children's baby books. Instead I look in flea markets, junk shops, garage sales, and dusty country stores, pursuing Depression-era glassware. Who knows why? Probably there is no single answer why some adult adoptees search, and adopting parents need to be aware that it may happen without misreading its intent.

The birth family's perspective. Another set of memories and another point of view confound Search questions. For every adult adoptee, there is one birth parent (or two) who participated either voluntarily or under pressure in relinquishment of a child for adoption. We are beginning to hear much more from these parents.

One group of mothers were teenage, unmarried, and of

middle-class background. Prior to the Supreme Court *Stanley* v. *Illinois* decision, which granted some rights to birth fathers, few men participated in adoption decisions unless they were married to the birth mother. These girls frequently went to live in maternity homes or with relatives, usually with their parents' help. They concealed their pregnancies from their home communities, bore their babies, placed them for adoption, and returned to their previous lives. Serious attempts were usually made to counsel the girls, but it is probably true that in many cases there was considerable pressure from families and society in favor of adoption. In the social climate of the day, adoption seemed the best alternative for mother and baby. Some of these girls never saw their babies and had little information about the adoption placement.

As late as 1970, nine out of ten pregnant teenagers who were not married placed their babies for adoption. By 1984, according to *Child Welfare*, only one in twenty pregnant adolescents placed their children for adoption. The changing social climate this reflects has now made it possible for many birth mothers of the 1950s and 1960s to identify themselves. Some spoke of guilt and misery over their secret and an unending sense of loss. From the viewpoint of greater maturity, some condemned the adults who they felt pressured them into a bad decision. Others confirmed that the decision was right at the time but now felt it was proper to break the silence and restore contact with their grown-up children. Many members of national Search groups come from these teenagers of the last generation. They are articulate, educated, and successful women who want to have a positive impact in the adoption picture for others, as well as settle Search issues for themselves.

Some birth parents who have gone public with their problem are troubled by the long-ago adoption because they are convinced that economic pressures, unfair court procedures, or other circumstances beyond their control caused the loss of their child. They want that wrong righted, either for them personally or by effecting changes in the system that can prevent like situations for others. The system is listening to this perspective, and many children who would have been cleared for adoption in an earlier time are now supported in their birth families.

In other cases babies were placed for adoption because of inadequate home situations of the young mothers. In many of these situations the alcoholism, poverty, or other problems of the families were never corrected, and the problems have continued into the current generation. The surfacing of some of these parents and the impact of their continuing problems upon the lives of adoptive parents and adoptees have considerable potential for pain and disruption.

There is another perspective in the birth-parent picture, but by its very nature it is less heard. Though the voices are anonymous, they are men and women who view the adoption they participated in as absolutely final. They have concealed this action, and the re-appearance in their lives of an adopted child is not desired. They ask that any changes in the system respect the compact they made to relinquish the child in return for privacy. Usually they support voluntary registries for those who wish to be identified and oppose opening of sealed records. In today's social climate this is sometimes pictured as selfish, reflecting again society's valuing of openness and its possibilities over privacy and the other values it protects.

The adoptive family's perspective. As adoptive parents ourselves, this section should be the easiest to write, but it is not. For we find our perspective changing as we consider what we know of one child's situation and what we don't know of another's. We think of foster children who were placed for adoption from our home and the varying circumstances they would meet if records were unsealed. We see possibilities for pain and misery for some, which the adoption was planned to mitigate. There is no one perspective for us, but we perhaps can reflect what kinds of issues we and other adoptive parents struggle to understand.

Many adoptive parents feel the current questioning of procedures means that society and birth parents are trying to renege on their agreements. They accepted parental responsibilities in return for parental benefits. Now the agency or the court or the birth parent or someone else is changing the rules to diminish those benefits. There may be a sense of betrayal of tremendously important trust.

One of these benefits was seen to be a lifelong commitment. Our society assumes that parents will care for children, and in a similar way children will provide love and emotional support to them in their middle and old age. The suggestion that adoptive parents should provide exclusively for the child in his developmental years, but share or lose entirely to others his companionship and support through his adulthood, strikes them as unfair. In their eyes it makes adoption very much second-class parenthood and more like a period of guardianship.

Adoptive parents also fear exploitation of a young adult and the adoptive family. They are aware that society sometimes removes children from families because there is a very disturbed birth mother or father. Sometimes there are siblings who would lean heavily on a newly found brother or sister. Recognizing that even the stable among us is vulnerable, and idealistic young people especially so, adoptive parents fear that manipulative or excessively dependent adults will take advantage of this young man or woman. They don't want that to happen and may feel either realistically concerned or overly protective.

The adoptive parents also experience anxiety that too much attention to future possibilities may interfere in the child's present relationships. Adolescents and even younger children often express intentions to find their birth parents when they are feeling most angry with the ones they have. Naturally this raises a question: "If I don't make the child happy, and he knows finding them is possible, will he just bide his time and run?" In the past adoptive parents could count on permanently sealed records to help provide the barrier while they struggled with parenting: "It's us or nobody." Some adoptive parents are not sure they can manage without that barrier. Because we have adopted older children, they have always known they could choose birth parents at some point. We have handled this issue by saying in various ways, "Yes, you can find and choose them, and when you are of age we'll help you do that if you want to. But for now we are the only parents you have, and we have to learn to live together on that basis."

Bringing Perspectives Together

It seems unlikely that solutions to Search dilemmas that are totally satisfactory to all will be found. We would like to suggest some probabilities and possibilities that we think are likely to emerge. Then each of us must plan our roles in the best way we can.

The move to open records will continue. Modifications regarding age limits, who can see them, and under what circumstances, will be worked out state by state, and all parties to adoption should try to have their views represented in the compromises. Probably *no one* should offer or rely on a promise of absolute confidentiality in adoption proceedings today.

Courts are not well suited to handle difficulties in personal relationships but are heavily involved in Search questions at present. The adage "hard cases make bad laws" applies. All members of Search controversies have much to gain by reaching compromises before judgments are handed down by courts. These rulings often lead to precedent setting, which can interfere with flexible handling of other situations.

Those who search and those who help them agree that times of stress in the adoption are bad times to engage in an active Search. When possible, difficulties in the adoptive relationship should be handled first. Naturally some Search issues are very much part of current problems in adoption, and these aspects may need to be pursued together. The assumption underlying this paragraph is that any relationship with birth parents is different and additional to the adoptive-parent relationship, not its replacement.

Solutions to Search dilemmas will be multiple. At the least we may need two definite tracks—one for adoptions completed by the old rules and one for current practice. Within these two general lines there must also be room for flexibility. In past practice, for example, a young teenager might be almost rigidly discouraged from even looking at the baby she planned to relinquish. Now some social workers are almost equally convinced that a birth mother should confirm her decision by a good-bye visit with her new baby. Procedures that take precedence over individual preferences and differences can lead to emotional and other difficulties for the parties involved, no matter how well intentioned or theoretically sound.

There are social implications in the potential changes that permeate far beyond the purposes we had in mind. The agencies and other professionals are best prepared to understand and project these into the discussion. Without insensitivity to individuals involved, we must consider social benefits and losses as we make changes. We live in a time of great emphasis on individual liberties and benefits. Someone must speak for the needs and rights of communities. If adoption becomes less final in the minds of children and parents, will disrupted adoptions become more frequent? The costs go beyond personal hurt and affect social welfare. If ties are weakened between adoption agencies and their clients because they cannot keep promises of confidentiality, will faith in our institutions be eroded further? We can make changes, but we must make them thoughtfully.

A child, though he is given to the care, custody, and control of parents, is not a possession. We cannot parcel him out for shares, even if we wanted to. More than love and duty binds families together. The glue is shared experiences as well. Families have demonstrated that they can accommodate a wide diversity of arrangements and multiple kinds and degrees of love. We do not need to be afraid to share love, for what we give we more than receive again. In matters of love, too, "with what measure you give it shall be given to you, full measure, pressed down, heaped up and shaken together." It will be so in adoption.

10

Looking Backward and Forward

Adoption, for some, is looking backward and remembering the joys, sorrows, trials, and triumphs of taking a child and seeing that child grow to adulthood. For others, it is looking back to see the plan that was worked out in your own life as you became a member of a second family. For many of you reading this book, adoption means looking forward to the whole process of making a decision and moving forward to translate that decision into welcoming a real child into your home. In each of these perspectives there is some pain, some anxiety, and some joy. In this chapter we would like to summarize two important aspects of adoption. These are that adoption is a lifetime commitment and that adoption has great joy and satisfaction.

A Lifetime Commitment

Many of the commitments we have in life are temporary. Some are semi-permanent in that they endure for a long time. These commitments can only be broken with pain, but they *can* be broken. We can decide to leave a company after many years of dedicated work and support. We can decide to leave a particular congregation. The fact that these commitments are semi-permanent makes them enduring but breakable.

The relationship of mother-child or father-child is permanent. We may emotionally withdraw or even disown a child, but he or she is still our son or daughter, and we can never change that. Once adoption is completed it is for life! The relationship is permanent and the commitments must be permanent also. This frame of mind is important in adoption. There may be times when you secretly wish you had not started the process, and it will only be due to the commitments you made that you can stick in there. At some point, in anger, the child may say, "You are not my real parent," and you must be ready to say, "Adoption makes me your *real* parent and it's for life!" One parent responded to our question about the joys of adoption by saying:

> Even though there are times when we feel we maybe can't go on, or we question why we started over with rearing a young child in our late thirties, we know God gave us our son as a special gift—and with God's help we will go on and some day look back on these years and think, "Wow! What a long haul those years were, but worth every tear, sorrow, joy, and prayer that went into them." He's our son and no one can ever change that.

Joy and Satisfaction

For the vast majority of adopting parents, the years from the thought of adoption to an adult son or daughter bring many joys and much satisfaction. It is clear from studies of adoption that joys outweigh sorrows and satisfactions outweigh dissatisfactions for adopting families. This is not to say there are no problems or trials, but the general reaction of a large majority of adoptive parents is: "It was all worth it!" In Kadushin's study of parents who had adopted older children, more than 70 percent of the parents expressed twice as many satisfactions with the adoption as dissatisfactions. Almost two-thirds of the parents expressed five satisfactions for every one dissatisfaction.

In Kadushin's summary of adoption-outcome studies, 74 to 83 percent of the adoptions had been rated "successful." Since most of these studies were on families in which there was an adoption of an older child, the figures are probably conservative estimates for all adopting families. We would expect them to be even higher for families where an infant was adopted. Kadushin found that 67 percent of the parents said they would do it all again and said that without hesitation. This is a higher rate of enthusiasm than Ann Landers seems to get from parents in general!

To find out what joys there are in adoption, we asked a group of adoptive parents what caused the most joy in their adoption. The results were very similar to the most-often-mentioned satisfactions of parents in Kadushin's study. The most frequently mentioned satisfactions were the child himself, the relationship to the extended family, the parent-child relationship, and the job of parenthood.

The Child

The most frequent source of *both* satisfaction and dissatisfaction in adoption is the child, but the satisfactions outweigh the dissatisfactions. Parents said, "God gave us a beautiful little toddler." Another parent said, "John and Joe are very lovable children. They make us happy just being around them." A third parent said, "Sharing in the lives of the children was the most happy thing about the adoption."

The Relationship with Extended Family

Many parents found joy and satisfaction in the fact that the adopted child was accepted by and in turn accepted the extended family. The joy of grandparents and the positive relationships between adopted siblings and between biological and adopted siblings were sources of joy and satisfaction. One parent said it was joy "seeing the children grow and being able to share the home life with them and now with our grandchildren."

Another said, "Getting a 'newborn' eight days old was like having our own." Parents also said things like "The child has brought much joy to my mother and father." One adopted adult said, "My aunt, who had never married, took a special shine to me as a child. She always made a point of making me feel I was special to her, and we developed a very close relationship that continues."

The joys and satisfactions are truly a family affair, and for many parents the extended joy brings a great measure of satisfaction to the whole adoption.

Parent-Child Relationships

Another source of joy and satisfaction is the relationship between parent and child. This is different from joy in the child as a person in that people can rejoice in the growth and accomplishments of an individual without talking about the relationship. Joy in the relationship comes from the close bond of love and affection that many parents have with their child. For some, this starts at the beginning. One mother said that the adoption was joy because it "fulfilled my almost desperate need to have a child of my *own*." Another noted the joy and satisfaction in "being able to share one life with another member and knowing it was *God's* will." One mother said the most happy experience was "while putting our seven-year-old to bed about two weeks ago. She has been our daughter since she was five months old. I looked down and saw tears in her eyes. I asked her what was the matter. Her reply: 'I am so glad my mother didn't abortion me, so she could give me to someone else who really cares. I know you really care for me.'"

The caring, loving relationship of parent-child can provide joy and satisfaction that is difficult to match.

The Job of Parenthood

Many adoptive parents found joy and satisfaction in fulfilling the responsibilities of parents and particularly in watching and helping a child grow and develop. One parent noted the satisfaction of knowing that their son likely would have ended up in prison if it had not been for the adoption. Another said it was joy simply "feeling we have given one person a home." A mother said, "Her becoming what she is now has been a joy to our hearts." You can almost feel the joy and satisfaction as you visualize that parent looking at her beautiful grown daughter.

Joy and sorrow, satisfaction and trials, are all a part of child rearing. They are also a part of rearing an adopted child. But the joys stick out the most. Would adoptive parents do it again? The resounding answer is: "You bet we would!"

Bibliography

Books

Benet, Mary Kathleen. *The Politics of Adoption*. New York: Free Press, 1976.

> A personalized look at adoption from an historical point of view. More helpful in the issues raised than the solutions posed.

Carney, Ann. *No More Here and There*. Chapel Hill, N.C.: University of North Carolina Press, 1976.

> Mother's record of first year with an adopted first-grader, plus an epilogue four years later. Realistic picture of one older-child adoption.

Comer, J. P., and Poussaint, Alvin F. *Black Child Care: How to Bring Up a Healthy Black Child in America*. New York: Simon and Shuster, 1975.

> Good resource for parents adopting a black child and for professional development with respect to special issues of black childrearing. (Author Pouissant is advisor to *The Cosby Show*.)

Jewett, Claudia. *Adopting the Older Child*. Cambridge, Mass.: Harvard Common Press, 1978.

Readable and practical summaries of actual adoptions to illustrate creation of parent-child relationships.

Kempe, R. S. and C. H. *Child Abuse*. Cambridge Mass.: Harvard University Press, 1978.
   Comprehensive study and recommendations on nature, effects, and incidence of child abuse. Good information for those adopting formerly abused children.

Ladner, Joyce. *Mixed Families*. Garden City, N.Y.: Doubleday, 1977.
   Excellent study of trans-racial adoption based on the literature and interviews with families in the United States who adopted across racial boundaries.

Lasnick, Robert S. A *Parent's Guide to Adoption*. N.Y.: Sterling Publishing Co., 1979.
   Emphasizes legal issues, and its appendix contains a copy of the Revised Uniform Adoption Act and the Model State Subsidized Adoptive Act.

Lifton, Jean. *Twice Born*. New York: McGraw Hill, 1975.
   Poetic, inconclusive, emotional. Example of Search books being written, but probably not typical of adoption experience. Helps in understanding adults who are spearheading Search emphases.

Martin, Cynthia D. *Beating the Adoption Game*. San Diego: Oaktree Publications, 1980.
   How to find your own baby. Examines her ideas from a Christian ethical perspective.

Meezan, William, Katz, Sanford, Usso, Eva Manoff. *Adoptions Without Agencies*. New York: Child Welfare League of America, 1980.
   Comprehensive study of characteristics of independent adoptions. Includes policy recommendations.

Sorosky, Arthur D., M.D.; Baron, Annette, MSW; and Pannor, Reuben, MSW. *The Adoption Triangle*. New York: Doubleday, 1978.
   A helpful contribution to understanding the feelings and attitudes of adult adoptees and birth parents.

Van Regenmorter, John and Sylvia, and McIlhaney, Joe S., Jr., M.D. *Dear God, Why Can't We Have a Baby?* Grand Rapids: Baker, 1986.
   Discusses the physical, emotional, and moral aspects of infertility from a Christian perspective.

Journal Articles

Most of the following articles were published in *Child Welfare*, the journal of the Child Welfare League of America. You will find many other timely articles on adoption in this bi-monthly journal.

Baran, Annette, et al. "Open Adoption." *Social Work* 21 (No. 2, March 1976): 97–100.

> Looks at adoption history in the United States and presents the case for open adoption.

Jones, Charles E., and Else, John F., "Racial and Cultural Issues in Adoption." *Child Welfare* 58 (No. 6, June 1979): 373–382.

> Asks important questions for parents considering adoption of a child of another race or culture.

Kadushin, Alfred. "Myths and Dilemmas in Child Welfare." *Child Welfare* 56 (No. 3, March 1977): 141–153.

> Good historical perspective on adoption.

Kim, Don Soo. "How They Fared in American Homes: A Follow-up of Adopted Children in the United States." *Children Today* (Washington, D.C.: Dept. of Health & Human Services) 6, (No. 2, March-April 1977): 2–6, 36.

> Major findings of a follow-up study in cooperation with Holt International Agency. Includes policy recommendations.

Littner, Nir. "Separation Reactions in the Educational Setting." *Child Welfare* 57 (No. 2, February 1979): 89–96.

> Material to help parents and teachers understand one possible source of school difficulty for a child who was older when adopted.

Mech, Edmund V. "Pregnant Adolescents: Communicating the Adoption Option." *Child Welfare* 65 (No. 6, November-December 1986): 555–567.

> Describes work in Illinois agencies toward consistently presenting adoption as an option for pregnant adolescents (less than 5 percent currently place their babies for adoption).

Spencer, Marietta E. "The Terminology of Adoption." *Child Welfare* 58 (No. 7, July 1979): 451–459.

A vocabulary to use in adoption. Worth learning.

Ward, Margaret. "Adoption of a Large Sibling Group." *Child Welfare* 57 (No. 4, April 1978): 233–241.

Mrs. Ward describes her experience and makes recommendations as the adopting mother of the sibling group. She is also a board member of a Canadian Children's Aid Society.

Addresses for Information

OURS, Inc., 3307 Highway 100 N., Suite 203 Minneapolis, MN 55422.

North American Council on Adoptable Children, NACAC Resource and Membership Office, 3900 Market St., Suite 247, Riverside, CA 92501.

Holt Adoption Agency, P.O. Box 2420, Eugene, OR 97402.

National Resolve, P.O. Box 474, Belmont, MA 02178.